GATHERINGS

GATHERINGS

FAVORITE WRITINGS BY

ELAINE CANNON

BOOKCRAFT
SALT LAKE CITY, UTAH

Library of Congress Cataloging-in-Publication Data

Cannon, Elaine.
  Gatherings : favorite writings by Elaine Cannon / Elaine Cannon.
    p. cm.
  Includes bibliographical references (p.).
  ISBN 1-57008-708-3
    1. Christian life—Church of Jesus Christ of Latter-day Saints authors. I. Title.

BX8656 .C323 2000
289.3'32—dc21

00-020246

Printed in the United States of America   18961-6588

10   9   8   7   6   5   4   3   2

CONTENTS

PUBLISHER'S PREFACE

After writing more than fifty books, author Elaine Anderson Cannon shares in one place the stories, talks, essays, and quotes that have meant the most to her. *Gatherings* is a collection of Sister Cannon's favorite writings, and is full of stories from the author's life and from the lives of those with whom she has come in contact throughout the years. It is a book for every reader. Certainly, if you have ever had a problem or an important decision to make, or if you have needed a change of perspective in life as a parent, grandparent, child, friend, or neighbor, this book will help. In its pages readers will also discover an exceptional lady, who has steadfastly taught through the written word that the gospel is a way of life.

"I'm a writer," says Sister Cannon. "It has ever been so. I was seventeen when I first started to write professionally (for money that is), and I haven't stopped since." Through six children, numerous Church callings, a long and rewarding marriage, and many personal trials, Elaine

Cannon has remained one of the most popular and endearing writers of the Latter-day Saint people. Her messages to youth, women, and Church leaders throughout the world are full of gospel truths and inspiring ideals.

Sister Cannon grew up on Capitol Hill in Salt Lake City, Utah, and witnessed the Depression years of the thirties as well as the frightening days of World War II. She graduated from West High School and attended the University of Utah, where she received a degree in sociology and worked her way through college as the society and women's editor at the *Deseret News*. She married D. James Cannon in the Salt Lake Temple on March 25, 1943. In stair-step order, six children were welcomed into the Cannon home. During the early years of their marriage, Sister Cannon found time to work out of her home by writing a column—every day for thirty years—for Intermountain newspapers. In the meantime, her children grew, as did she through numerous Church callings and educational experiences. She served as associate editor of Church magazines for youth and their leaders and contributed regularly to national magazines, including *Better Homes and Gardens* and *Seventeen*.

In 1978 she was called as general president of the Young Women, where she served for six years. This calling allowed her to travel throughout the world, meeting hundreds of humble individuals from all walks of life. The people she met have contributed to her life and her work. "The sum of those people," she says, "is what I am." Through her travels she learned what she now believes is the message of her life: "Draw on the power of heaven. Claim your blessings. Serve where the Lord asks."

This message shines through in each of her more than fifty published books, as does her hope that the readers of her books will be blessed by the personal experiences and everyday life events about which she writes. "I have had a personal witness," she says, "that life is better with your hand in the Lord's. I want my readers to feel that."

Surely, readers of this book will recognize that Elaine Cannon has kept her hand in the Lord's throughout her own life.

MARRIAGE
AND FAMILY

---

*Families are God's way of blessing the world,
of shaping a strong, stubborn man into a strong,
sensitive father, and a beautiful, bossy woman
into a beautiful, blessed mother.*

AN EGGBEATER
IN THE SILVER CHEST?

To the brides and grooms we say, since you've fallen in love some changes have come. You two who were friends now look at each other and the world around you with an eye single to your own needs. Out of all the faces in the world, this one face is your kind of face; this one smile, the warming one.

You build your dreams, set the date, and go through the motions of betrothal. And while that enchanting spell spreads over you, the wedding date finally comes; and you two, holding hands, walk off into the sunset to live happily ever after.

New in your discovery of each other's delightful qualities is the discovery of each other's ways in the daily tasks of life. You are full of wonder, all right; but you wonder, too, how you could not have suspected that this marvelous skier would decorate the bedroom with socks, boots, and used lift passes. And when he dries the dishes, he absentmindedly puts the eggbeater in the silver chest.

He, meanwhile, wonders how you, his beautiful and

3

adorable wife, could possibly emerge as a toothpaste-tube mutilator, a cap leaver-offer, a financial hazard with the checkbook. What's more, you washed his whites with a red sock entangled.

Now the wonder may turn to wondering whether two people so different, though once cloaked in love, can ever become one.

It is at such moments of wonder that you can feel glad that you are friends as well as husband and wife. You can be thankful for happy memories and precious investments of time together. You're grateful for an understanding of God's plan of life and the potentiality of the human spirit. In all of your differences there is one important quality you two share—imperfection and the right to personal improvement. And you've made a commitment.

So in sweet patience—a patience that grows in the practice of it—you try again: she picks up the socks; he replaces the toothpaste cap; she retrieves the eggbeater; he copes with the overdraft one more time. Then you kiss each other in a new kind of loving. The happily-ever-after idea becomes a stronger possibility instead of a romantic myth.

There is a classic bit of Christmas literature, "The Gift of the Magi," by O. Henry that ideally describes giving to each other. It is the story of the poverty-stricken lovers who had no gifts to give at the Christmas season. Finally the wife, whose beautiful long hair was indeed her crowning glory, had her hair cut to sell; and she used the money to buy a platinum chain for her husband's prized possession, his gold watch. He, in similar unselfishness, sold his treasured timepiece to buy a pair of tortoise-shell combs for his wife's cascade of brown hair. It is a tender story. Their unselfish gifts made them grow in love.

Perhaps you two aren't the perfect partners yet. But you're in good company, and you keep on trying because you promised you would. You are two imperfect children of God who now look at each other and the world around you with an eye single to another's needs.

You are friends and lovers still. What, after all, does an eggbeater in the silver chest have to do with anything?

What would we do without children?
Well, for starters, nothing!

WHAT IS A FAMILY?

Years ago Allen Beck started something when he wrote two charming pieces called "What Is a Boy?" and "What Is a Girl?" Today we'll take a look at what a family is—with apologies to Mr. Beck.

A family is God's way of blessing the world.

A family keeps a mother from doing the things she's always wanted to do until she is too old to do them. But somewhere along the way a family weaves such a magic that one day Mother realizes that this, after all, *is* what she wanted to do all along.

Families are always multiplied by two and come in a wide range of mathematical combinations. This unique variety pack comes in assorted sizes, shapes, colors, dispositions, and bank accounts. Each additional member to the unit challenges, for a time, the lofty premise that all men are created equal—that newcomer gets more attention per hour than everyone else put together.

As we look at the individual components, it is easy to see what makes families exactly the way they are. From the youngest to the eldest, each member has a part to play.

The youngest member of the circle is termed the baby. This has nothing to do with age, actually, but rather a stage of being; for whether six months or sixty years old, the youngest child is persistently referred to as "the baby."

Babies are for picking—picking at, picking up, and picking up after. Babies are also for kissing and caring and diapering and for bedding and bottling, for holding and hugging.

They come equipped with an amazing gift for melting the most rugged father into a reasonable facsimile of jelly and convincing a mother that she'd rather have her hands in detergent than suntan oil any day.

Babies cause parents to love each other more deeply, to smile more through tears, to buy more film, lose more sleep, stay home from more parties, and become more painful bores. But they also remind them that heaven is really very close after all.

Yes, babies are for loving.

The next age group in the family is the toddlers. These little destroying angels may be found wherever there is water. They are also known to slide down the best furniture, sneeze when fed, and move restlessly from room to room, leaving their trail behind them. The only time they are quiet is when they are doing something they shouldn't. Toddlers have a disarming way of charming. They smile their sweetest smiles when they are about to be disciplined.

Toddlers are on the threshold of a great new world of learning. So toddlers are for teaching—teaching to sing, to pray, to read, to eat with forks instead of fingers, to understand that training pants are the road to freedom, to know right from wrong, and to recognize the difference between Jesus and Santa Claus. One of the nicest things about a toddler is that he loves you unabashedly, anyway.

Oh, toddlers are for loving.

Then there is that delightful stage when offspring can now advance to the nearest grade school. Grade schoolers are famous for giggles and gum, for the blank spaces in the front of their smiles, for freckles sprinkled generously across the bridge of the nose, and for telling family secrets to neighbors.

They have a talent for running—running noses, running away and running errands, and for running the bathroom water the longest with the least to show for it. They are for getting—measles at Christmas, and into trouble when you aren't looking. They are skilled at getting things into drawers already too full, and other things out of closets that shouldn't have been opened in the first place. They ask more questions and eat more times a day than you had in mind. They are just great at losing boots, sweaters, one glove, balls, books, lunch pails, and instructions. They are devoted to creatures of the earth that growl, slither, wiggle, or crawl. Grade schoolers have been known to collect bottles, rocks, wrappers, and a fan club made up of proud parents and grandparents, of teachers and big sisters, especially when they perform in the school program.

Oh, grade schoolers are for loving.

Teenagers in the family grow too much too soon or too little too late. They make us proud with their beauty of body, quickness of wit, fierce loyalties, and the fact that they remembered our birthday with an extravagant gift without being told.

They are the challenge and the challenger. They challenge our authority, our decisions, our lifestyle, our system, our taste in music, and our turn to have the car.

They emerge smarter, stronger, and more spiritual than we. But let us remember that we lifted—dragged, fought, loved?—them to where they are today. We just won't talk about it in front of them—it would ruin the whole thing.

Yes, families are God's way of blessing the world, of shaping a strong, stubborn man into a strong, sensitive father, and a beautiful, bossy woman into a beautiful, blessed mother.

Families are for loving each other anyway. Yes, a family is God's way of blessing the world. Oh, thank God, families are forever!

A TURNING POINT

Turning points can be a blessing. Often they come in life when a lesson is learned or a trial is tackled.

Turning points get a person going a different direction, feeling another way, changing a perspective.

When I was a young mother I was building my dream life. It was a dream life because it had little to do with reality. I dreamed that at least once a week children and mother were lovely looking, charming, scintillating people seated around a bountiful and beautiful Sunday table with the handsome patriarch presiding in dignity and grace. That is how I dreamed the perfect life would be each Sunday. What went on during the week was another matter, but Sundays were supposed to be perfect.

Reality at that time was that we'd had a baby about every year, whether we needed one or not, until there was a houseful of little destroying angels who didn't understand my dream. There were five of them under seven, and their very young father was a bishop. He didn't understand my dream either. My husband did the best he could to juggle watching over his Church flock by day and night and especially on Sunday, and trying to be a father of his own brood whenever he could.

The real problem for me and my dream was that he was always late getting home on Sundays. I used to get very discouraged with the whole arrangement. Once I had a fever of 104 degrees and no husband to help me because he was visiting the sick. I recall wondering how sick one had to be to get the bishop to visit. Several times I considered making an appointment on Sunday to see this bishop, my husband.

There was one particular Sunday that was a turning point for me in that era of my life. The children and I came home from church to the table I'd set in its Sunday best the night before. The traditional Sunday dinner was ready, and the little ones were anxious—but Daddy hadn't returned yet. We waited and waited and waited. Finally my dream was totally shattered by tired cries and hunger pains. I fed them little meals and helped them go down for their naps. Then I waited some more, becoming more frustrated, disillusioned, heartbroken, and furious by the moment. I worried some about why he hadn't called, but that didn't help. Pacing hadn't brought that bishop-husband-daddy home, and neither had children's tears nor my own angered spirit.

Then there came the turning point for me. I noticed my hunger. Hours had passed, and I hadn't eaten. I was certain my six-foot, six-inch partner in life had not eaten either. I was reassured that he'd have come home to eat, if for no other reason, if he possibly could have! I prayed for his well-being, then ate, and settled down for a nap of my own.

I was awakened by his kiss. By then my spirit had sweetened and my attitude changed. I welcomed him warmly. I fussed over him and fed him and cupped my chin in my hands to watch him while he silently ate. When at last the meal was over, he turned to me and said seriously, "Elaine, before coming home today I had the most spiritual experience of my life as a bishop. A miracle happened, right while I was blessing someone. If you had spoiled it by sulking or scolding me when I showed up, I'd have been so disappointed I'd have had a hard time getting over it. Thank you for understanding. I've never loved you more."

I smiled and said nothing, but panic struck me inside—what if I had blown that? Inside I prayed my thanks to Heavenly Father that I got hungry and then smart enough to calm down and not be a spoiler.

It was a turning point. I turned away from selfish dreams to support my husband in his unselfish service to others. And I felt very good about it.

That was a beginning in a long life of coming to grips with priorities, of balancing along the fine line between good choices and better ones.

Peace usually begins at home and advances to reconciliation with God. But the other way around works just as well. Find peace with God, and one can't rest until wrongs are righted at home. Then that place becomes a heaven on earth, and all who sit at the table are as if at the Lord's Supper.

TRUE BEAUTY

My family and I were new in a neighborhood, and I had just met a fine gentleman with whom I'd be serving in a Church assignment. We were visiting in the foyer of the chapel when I asked him when I would get to meet his wife.

"Now," he said. "Why wait? You are in for a treat!"

"Wonderful," I returned. "Where is she?"

"She's in the cultural hall."

So were a dozen other women I didn't know yet, who were decorating for a church bazaar.

"How will I know her?"

"Easy!" He was exuberant. "Go in there and look for the most beautiful woman in the room—that's my wife." Then he gave me a few more details and I left. I entered the room looking for a lady who was a cross between Sophia Loren and a young Audrey Hepburn. What I saw were mothers of many, empty nesters, and some fine Molly Mormons. I didn't see one who answered his descriptions at all. Finally I asked someone and she pointed out the man's wife.

As I think about this woman now, I can think only of beauty and loveliness. Honestly. I know her as one of the finest women I've ever met. I love her for her great kindness to me over the years. But at that moment I was shocked. There must be some mistake! Not only was the woman who had been pointed out to me no movie star but she also had few redeeming features. I noticed that she had gentle curls of fine mahogany hair, a light in her eyes, and a warm smile. But that was it. Her eyes were unusually wide set. Her lips were thick, surrounding an ugly overbite. Her ears were prominent. Her nose, however, was the nose of a movie star—Bob Hope! But that smile and those eyes, when I introduced myself, obliterated imperfect features.

Of course he loved her. He'd lived with her. He'd shared pillow talk. She had been told that she was beautiful and desirable so many times that *she was!* He'd been the object of her incredibly generous service and her unequivocal support. That woman would crawl through a forest of prickly trees and tangleweeds to help her man. Of course he loved her.

THE BLESSINGS OF MARRIAGE

It is sometimes easier to develop satisfaction in one's own marriage, even if it may have been sagging for some years, than to ever find satisfaction in a second try— let alone in an extramarital relationship, no matter how tempting. Even the smallest effort put forth in marriage can often bring immediate rewards. This may be because we aren't alone in working toward the goal.

As members of the Church, we believe that marriage is ordained of God. We believe that the Lord will keep his promises to help us, and that he is bound when we do what he says. If there are children involved, all the more reason to nurture and strengthen a marriage. There is no one on earth so interested in the offspring of you two than you two! Count on that. That's why divorced couples with children are never really free from each other. The interaction goes on and on to the grave. Just ask around. Maybe a troubled marriage is the very place and time to begin counting blessings—naming what you do have going for you, what does pull you together—instead of negatively living with a list of complaints.

Looking elsewhere for happiness is tantamount to walking one step closer to the devil's zone. To view one's marriage with an attitude of "Is this all there is?" is to degrade one's own ability to make decisions, to change behavior, to maturely live the gospel of Jesus Christ. Look at it this way: You two are God's children. You are spirit brother and sister who happen to be bound together in marriage. You can learn (albeit with God's substantial help) to live in peace until love surfaces again. Begin on the basis of counting blessings and drawing satisfaction from all the hills you've climbed together and all that you've invested in. It takes two to teeter-totter. Start with a discussion about blessings. Make your list one by one. If you were alone together on a desert island, what would you have to work a miracle of joy? Questions like "How can I please my spouse?" and "How has my spouse pleased me?" open a new category of blessing counting.

Karina and Wayne were on the verge of divorce, notwithstanding their four children under six years of age. In a last-chance effort, they attended a Church Continuing Education Week in their community. A prominent woman lecturer from Salt Lake conducted one of the discussions.

One night this teacher explained that she was prompted by the Spirit to change her subject. After the class, Karina confessed to the teacher that this class was an answer to prayer. Karina had been fasting and praying that a miracle would happen that night. It had! Wayne had taken her hand and whispered in her ear his sorrow over his past attitude and behavior. He had begged her to give him another chance. This time, he said, they'd let the Lord in on their marriage.

Now their four children have grown up, filled missions, and married in the temple. At the recent wedding breakfast of the last child, both Karina and Wayne happily gave away the secret of their own successful marriage: pray together for help, and in gratitude acknowledge God's influence.

Friends are important, but when you have
a child you should turn into a parent.

BEGINNING THE
WORLD ALL OVER AGAIN

Thomas Paine wrote, "We have it in our power to begin the world over again." And for me, that is true each January—a chance to begin my world over again and keep an accounting of it in a personal journal.

The beginning of a new year is the time to start a new journal, even if the old one isn't quite finished. It is in keeping with the tradition of turning over a new leaf, or flipping the calendar back to the beginning.

In a new journal all the pages are clean, and the promise of better entries, better living, of surprise experiences lures one to the fresh start.

What will the new year hold? What challenges and simple delights? What separations and comings together? What lessons learned and mistakes made? What insights? What happenings to speak about? What witnesses of God's goodness of which to testify?

Ah, the gift of a new year is a blessed one. A clean,

unmarked, unlettered journal rests on the desk before us like a new life.

There is another reason to write a record, and that's so there is one to enjoy when the present becomes the past. A record underscores the memory—verifies it, even.

A certain woman was seventy-two when she died. At her funeral someone read the details of her birth, recorded in joy by her mother. At the end of her life here was proof and perspective about the beginning, about the reaching and helping and brightening of her seasons. At this dying a kind of resurrection occurred; for the whole family loved their sister and each other anew. Her younger brother, reading from journals on this occasion, turned the hearts of the family to each other. A written line or two became their lifeline to the dry farm, the small store mother kept, the loved ones at Christmas or at daily prayer, the father's Sunday ritual, the hard times, the faithful times, the laughing times, and the inevitable struggle to add a new room as yet another baby came.

It was a wonderful, rooted remembering, that funeral. There was no shriveling sadness, but only a heavy gathering of reasons for our being and then moving on.

It seems a testimony in itself for keeping a record of the proceedings of our days.

And here is another.

The teenage son was having trouble relating to his family. His thoughts and his behavior were cluttered with the onslaught of life that came at him as fast as the inches at the end of his legs. His mother's demands especially seemed a burden. He didn't know her anymore. He wasn't sure she understood him at all, and he was shocked to discover that after all she wasn't as perfect as he had thought her to be when he was much younger. His older sisters were to him mere replicas of the authority figure he resented in his mother.

Then one day he came upon his mother's open journal. Reading it was a temptation he couldn't resist. A perfunctory glance or two, almost a sneer, and then quiet as he turned the pages that revealed a spiritual side to his mother he hadn't appreciated. Soon uncomfortable tears were burning his cheeks. He learned from this irrevocable source that his mother loved him. He also realized that she prayed for him and that she was mindful of good things he had done. Then he read a note tucked inside, written by one of his sisters for Mother's Day. He'd never suspected that she was capable of such deep feeling. He was interested in reasons she expressed for loving their mother, reasons that simply hadn't occurred to him. The warmth filling his heart opened a door in his mind. He hadn't understood. This record taught valuable lessons at the very time he needed to learn them. He gained new insights in all inter-family relating. He mellowed under the security of such a blessing and of being loved. In return, he felt love for others freshen his soul again. For him the world began all over again.

We who would give our children everything, would even sacrifice our lives for them if need be, must consider the importance of keeping records that can enrich their lives beyond description and reach them beyond our voice.

Our posterity has a right to know their roots without scrounging for them and perhaps uncovering only part. Keeping records can assure them of this. Writing our life story can help them know their parents. Knowing brings understanding, and understanding strengthens love.

We'll want to write as fine and complete a record as we can. When we keep current accounts of our lives, we should preserve these and pass them on to the next generation, as we are inspired to, with instructions that our children are to add their own histories and records. Then all the accounts should be passed on to the next generation, who are to follow the same pattern in turn.

It is the Lord's way, and it is good.

The Bible says, "For whatsoever things were written aforetime were written for our learning, that we through patience and comfort of the scriptures might have hope" (Romans 15:4). This can be said of the things we write today. We build a kind of sacred supplement to the scriptures as we record our life, our testimony of Christ, our service, our struggles to learn for ourselves right and wrong.

From the land of me to the land of you is one way of describing all personal records: life stories, genealogical sheets, diaries, journals, photograph albums, and oral history tapes. What we record in our privacy can be read by posterity, in due time.

We train them in the traditions of their fathers. We keep the chain linking the generations unbroken. So, of course, will our posterity.

It's like beginning the world all over again.

I don't know about your children, but my offspring
understand heaven to be furnished with fast-food
stalls dispensing glazed donuts and chocolate milk.
Plus, they get a different mom.

A NECKLACE FOR MOM

Scott was eleven when he got a paper route. He had only one goal in mind: he loved his mother and wanted to buy her a really fine Christmas gift, and he wanted the independence of having his own money to do it with. So he delivered papers, collected the money, and stored the savings away in a quart-size canning jar, a jar over which he had glued pictures cut from magazines so that the contents of the jar would be private. He hid the jar deep in the clothing of his dresser drawer.

As the weeks and months passed, the little savings grew. Every so often, Scott would have to squish down the bills in order to fit more money in the jar. Finally, Christmas was close enough that he felt he could take the money down to Auerbach's Department Store and buy a gift.

He had been looking at necklaces, dresses, purses, vases, books, dishes, and perfume. He hadn't decided what he wanted until one day he saw a handsome necklace designed after the one that Elizabeth Taylor had worn in the movie *Cleopatra*. A picture of Elizabeth as Cleopatra was on display to promote the necklace. Scott thought that it was the prettiest necklace he'd ever seen on the world's most beautiful lady—except for his mother, of course. He was loyal to his mother. She could do justice to such an elaborate spray of stones on the Egyptian-styled collar necklace. But the gift would cost more than he had. He'd wait. He asked the clerk if she could save the necklace for him until future collections were gathered from the paper route. They made the arrangements, and she took some of his money as a down payment.

Scott was excited. The more he thought about the necklace the surer he became that he wanted it for his mother. He thought about how she had made his costume for the school play and had stayed up late nights to do it. He thought about the time he had injured his leg and she drove him back and forth between home and school, never grumbling. She had sat by his hospital bed and read wonderful stories to him, too. Mother could read aloud and recite the scriptures by heart with great expression. Oh, Mother was special!

Scott talked to the owner of a neighborhood bakery who then let Scott come in before school in the morning and help him by lifting heavy bags of flour for the day's baking. Those were cold mornings and bed seemed especially inviting, especially when his brothers were still sleeping. But then Scott would go in to kiss his mother good-bye and learn that she had already packed him a lunch for the day. She was worth this effort, and how surprised she would be to get this wonderful necklace, just like a movie star's—*a movie star and a queen!*

Shortly before Christmas, mother was suddenly taken to the hospital for serious surgery. There was a growth in the front of her neck, and the doctor made an incision at the base of her throat from under one ear across to the other. The family was frightened. They fasted together and had prayers morning and night. Daddy called the temple and asked them to put her name on the special prayer roll. Everybody helped around the house to try to take Mother's place. The school lunches were dry and laundry piled up, but the neighbors brought in good dinners, so the family managed to get along all right. But with Christmas coming and Mother sick, nothing seemed right.

Scott had kept his secret of the necklace to himself for many weeks but now thought he should get it from the store and give it to Mother right away—just in case she didn't get home for Christmas. To know how much her son loved her might help her feel better.

Scott's dad got permission from the doctor and the hospital staff to take Scott to Mother's hospital room. With his present in hand, his heart pounded with excitement. What a surprise!

He hurried into the elevator and then down the long hall with his dad struggling to keep up with him. How happy Mother would be!

No matter how many times Dad had asked Scott what the gift was, the boy wouldn't tell. This was his very own gift to Mother. And now the time had come to present it to her. Christmas Day itself couldn't be any better than this.

Scott hadn't seen Mother for two weeks. She had been too ill for children to come in. He was shocked at how thin and fragile she appeared. Her neck was bandaged, and she could hardly turn her head.

But Dad told Scott that he could give her a kiss on the forehead. The boy then placed the package on top of his mother's hands, folded across her waist. Daddy explained quickly that Mother's tears were because she was so happy to see him: she agreed with a small nod of her head. Scott stood at the foot of the bed, where they could see each other while she opened the gift. He was afraid to help her, to touch her. She seemed like a stranger to him. He was afraid he might hurt her, too. So Daddy helped her.

Off came the beautiful wrappings of silver and blue

that the clerk at Auerbach's had put on the box for him. Then the lid of the box came off—silver with pressed designs all over. Then Dad lifted the soft flat cotton square in the shape of the box. And there for Mother to see was the spray of silver, turquoise, and coral with long, gold teardrops evenly forming a Cleopatra collar.

Dad took the heavy necklace from its box and held it up for Mother to see. She gasped, "Scott! Where? . . . How much? . . . What did you do? . . . Oh, Scott!"

"I love you, Mother. I started to buy it before you were sick. You have to get better now, don't you see? I've been paying for it for three months! You just have to get better, don't you see?" Scott was crying now, too. Even Dad had to blow his nose.

"Oh, Scott, my darling," said Mother.

"Now you can't wear it! All those bandages," Scott suddenly realized.

"Ah, but I can hold it close to me all day and night until I *can* wear it!" explained Mother. And she did. Dad found a hospital blanket pin and, attaching it to the necklace, pinned it to Mother's gown. "One day very soon—maybe for Christmas, or maybe for my January birthday—I'll be able to wear it. I'll come home, Scott. Anybody who would buy me a gift like this deserves one more good lunch in his life, at least. I'm the mother who will fix it, too."

TRADITION

Families do things their own way on Christmas Day, and mostly that's how people want it to be, until somebody leaves home to marry—joining his or her roots with somebody else's.

Our family was an all-out family for Christmas, going for the full treatment within what budget and energy would allow. When we got in gear for the season, we were busy with much preparation in getting, giving, eating, decorating, and doing good deeds; we filled the house with good fragrance, good music, good art, and some well-loved but not-so-marvelous renderings from the elementary school days.

Other people do it other ways. You do it yours. And that is how it should be, of course. It's absolutely fine, in fact—unless one of the simple celebrators marries one of the all-out-for-the-whole-show people.

And that is exactly what happened in our family.

These two had been married for a few delightful

months when Christmas neared and our daughter asked her new husband when they could go and get their Christmas tree. He said they weren't going to get a tree. He came from a family of long-standing conservationists, and they didn't believe in destroying a forest for a pagan custom.

So much for Christmas as she had always known it. So much for "personal identity" for either of them if the argument ensued.

The day she called for a formal appointment with me I knew that trouble existed in the new nest. She talked of loving, wondering how she could love this man so much when they didn't agree on something so basic as a Christmas tree! I listened for a time and all the while wondered if we had done her a favor, after all, by making such a big celebration of Christmas.

When it was my turn to talk, I expressed my gratitude to her that she had loved growing up in our home, with our kind of celebration for the season of joy which marks the most important event in history. Then, I expressed gratitude for the very fine young man she had brought into our family. I was certain his good parents felt the same way about our "jewel." Clearly, this young man felt strongly about his own upbringing, his own family's understated celebration and traditions.

Background. Stalemate. Hard questions.

Could celebrations so different ever be reconciled! Could remembrances of how Christmas always had been be put aside for someone else's memories? Whose roots mattered most? Which celebration was better, more appropriate? Who was right?

I responded quickly to the last question, "Who is right?" to suggest my personal philosophy in these tight squeezes marriage presents to us: "Would you rather be right or loved?"

Finally, we talked about the right of each family to establish its own traditions. Family life was about compromise. When children enter into family life and grow up they bring even more change into the traditions that a couple has established. Unless people cooperate, unhappiness, argument, and even estrangement result.

Then we talked about traditions and symbols. Nothing sacred existed about how many verses were sung, of which carol, or how the turkey was stuffed. Whether the cranberries were sieved or served whole, plain or with grated orange, and whether the dressing was moist or dry crumbs, mattered little as well. Christmas really didn't depend on whether there was a tree. What it did depend upon was an abiding love in *their* home and happiness in what *they* were building. The day that those two were married, a new family began—an eternal, forever family was their goal. *That* family was not obligated to do things in exactly the way either of their parents had done. They were neither bound to celebrate sensibly if sparsely, nor foolishly and elaborately, nor somewhere in between. They could prayerfully and carefully talk things over (a procedure of marriage that needs another book to explain!), eventually deciding what counted for the two of them as they began the traditions of their family Christmases.

Well, they did that. It turned out that they had a tree, but one that came in a pot so that it could be planted in the garden in the spring!

Christlikeness brings more joy to the season of Christmas than pursuing one's personal identity. I may be at odds with the psychiatrists about the idea, but it seems that ideally the next step after a potted tree, or of some other symbol of the season, may well be that one partner will say to the other, "I love you more than a tree or a tradition. Let's do what will make *you* happy!"

And that is how I learned to like roast beef with rice instead of mashed potatoes and gravy! You win some and you lose some, but what is gained in the compromise is of more value.

"MAMA, YOU'VE GOT TROUBLE"

The tulips squeezed into the little fellow's fist were drooping, the stems where they had been twisted free from the mother plant were already beginning to string and curl, like dandelion stems we children used to deliberately suck in and blow out on to reshape.

"Mama, you've got trouble!" he said, thrusting the flowers toward her.

It was an appealing sight to this woman so grateful for motherhood, to see her bright little four-year-old and his constant companion of the same age, the neighborhood shepherdess from down the block, standing before her with their spring loot.

"Trouble? Not me," she answered. "I am one happy woman just having you here!" She snuggled the two children to her.

"Hey, Mom, the flowers—you'll mess them up. They're for you." The boy wiggled free and thrust the flowers toward her again. "Well, anyway, Mrs. Bertagnole says for me to tell you that you are in trouble."

"I am in trouble?" The unfamiliar tulips took on new meaning.

"Yes, because I picked all of these flowers. That's what she said. But I did it for you because you said you wanted some tulips, and we don't have any, and Mrs. Bertagnole had these white ones." He breathed a deep sigh and laid the tulips in his mother's lap.

She did have trouble. Why hadn't he gone next door to Troxlers' and picked tulips? the mother wondered. It wouldn't have mattered so much. They had half an acre of bright yellow and multistriped tulips that had been in the ground many years. But Mrs. Bertagnole really didn't grow flowers. Or children!

"Darling, these are beautiful tulips. But most of all I love you for thinking of me and for coming directly home with them. Thank you!" And she hugged him again and put her face in the graceful arch of the petals. "I love you for bringing me these beautiful tulips. Now about that trouble we seem to be in. Let's talk it over. First, you forgot to get permission from Mrs. Bertagnole to pick her tulips. Second, why don't we go together to see how we can make her feel better?"

"Mom, I'm glad you are my friend."

GOD PROVIDED A HELPMEET

I stand all amazed at how wonderful marriage is, despite the fact that so many marriages in our day end in divorce. If you believe the stats in the daily news you'd deplore the institution of marriage. But I have a whole host of friends my age who agree that marriage is very rewarding. They've hung in there all the way, climbing the dark mountains or shoving each other through the narrow passes. But golden anniversaries, here they come, tightly holding hands.

Holding hands? In gratitude? In love? In fear and trembling of separation?

All that and more.

Marriage is great because it lasts so long; because the investment is mighty and therefore must be harvested; because there isn't anyone in all the world who will care about your children as much as will their father. People not only hang on but many also make marriage sweeter as they learn the art and polish up their ability to pass from the fever of sexual curiosity to friendship without sacrificing love.

Here is something that can be helpful to your thinking. We women have heard often that God provided a "helpmeet" (spelled as two words in the scriptures) for man. You'll be highly enlightened, I believe, if you research the meaning of that word. For example, in my new dictionary, under the word *helpmeet,* is the following:

"*Usage:* The existence of the two words *helpmeet* and *helpmate,* meaning exactly the same thing, is a comedy of errors. God's promise to Adam, as rendered in the King James Version of the Bible, was to give him 'an help meet for him' (that is, a helper fit for him). In the 17th century the two words *help* and *meet* in this passage were mistaken for one word, applying to Eve, and thus *helpmeet* came to mean 'a wife.' Then in the 18th century, in a misguided attempt to make sense of the word, the spelling *helpmate* was introduced. Both errors are now beyond recall, and both spellings are acceptable" (*American Heritage Dictionary,* second college edition [Boston: Houghton Mifflin, 1990], p. 604).

Both spellings may be acceptable, sisters, but never forget the original meaning of *meet* in this context. It means someone fit, someone who joins because of appropriateness or worthiness!

Someone once said, "Adam came first, but Eve started it all!" And so she did. Now to wrap it up: "Eve," carefully, prayerfully, tenderly, joyfully, for as long as it takes, work with your "Adam."

Unless scripture study is the family pattern, trying to guide each other through contemporary Babylon and heartbreak is nigh impossible. It was true for our family when we were young parents, and it is true today for our children who are now parents with problems of their own. Everything changes, but nothing changes. If it were not so, family life would be like watching pro-football all New Year's Day with guests who don't understand the plays. Dismal. A parent might as well be speaking Farsi to the family or quoting Shakespeare to a group of kindergartners. They just don't get what you want them to.

THE ROCKER

Down the hill from the home of my childhood there lived a family who were hard hit by the financial crash of 1929. They were unlikely candidates for the wrenching of such an event since they were small-town people who scarcely had heard of stocks and bonds, much less owned any. But wrenched they were, caught in the wake of bank crashes and a depressed economy.

They had moved to Salt Lake so that the father could start a bricklaying business. For a time, all went well. The big house and the happy family were signs of his success. But then his business collapsed. They introduced the Depression to our neighborhood. And we all watched carefully, in sympathy, with curiosity, and under personal threat.

As the years passed they finally lost everything but each other, as the saying goes. In some families the "each other" part slips away as well, under the weight of hardship.

This family seemed to handle their depressed days well. Maybe that's one reason I remember them so clearly.

The day the living room plush sofa and armchair set and the Oriental rugs were carried away by the furniture store's company truck, I was there taking it all in. I was curled up on a wide brick wall that closed in the front steps and supported the balcony of the second story. It was amazing to note that tears rolled down the face of the father instead of the lady of the house. She bit her lip and narrowed her eyes—that was all. However, the next day she put a henna pack on her baby-soft hair. . . .

The red hair and the daily dusting and polishing of the hardwood floors in the living and dining rooms were brave gestures against deprivation. The hair was something less beautiful to my eyes, but those floors were impressive.

The only way into the rest of the house was through one end of the living room, where a little entrance hall was formed from the front door to the kitchen door and framed the railing of the stairs to the bedrooms. And there was a walk-in coat closet.

The furniture that was left in the living room included the Majestic radio, and a sturdy, tall-backed, oak rocker faced away from the shiny oak arches that separated the two front rooms. The living room flowed through these arches into the generous dining room that was windowed all around. We could see the Great Salt Lake on the horizon and the railroad tracks just a mile or two below the hill where we all lived. We noticed the view more with the rooms empty.

And we noticed those shiny hardwood floors. What an impact this had on me! So deeply did this situation affect my dreamtime that in every home my husband and I have lived in, polished hardwood floors have been an important feature.

There were other things this family had to live with,

besides the gleaming floors, of course. They had each other. There was a girl, who was my friend, and four or five husky boys who could swallow a quart of milk straight from the bottle in the Frigidaire. At one sitting they could make a super-sized yellow cake disappear, washing it down with whatever homemade root beer they could get their hands on. (The mother hid it all over the house.)

About that yellow cake . . .

Sometimes the grocer would let the mother have eggs and chocolate, and she'd bake one of her famous cakes. She'd make one for the grocer, too, because that's how she got the chocolate. He was a widower and would get a hankering for something sweet. She didn't have the money to buy luxuries like chocolate, so it was a good deal, and in the process I learned how to make yellow cake and real fudge frosting from scratch and by hand. That means without an electric mixer!

The day the cake was made was always a happy one. A drizzle of batter or frosting on a child's finger is a lovely treat.

The kitchen had furniture. The round oak extension table had been their grandmother's, so it wasn't taken away. There were assorted chairs that the boys straddled backwards at the table. We played Pit. They glued their balsawood model airplanes. We all shelled peas, and snapped beans from the garden, and cracked dried apricot pits to use as nuts in cookies. And one of the boys wrote endless, sticky rhymes on brown wrapping paper torn into sheets of sorts. They were sent farther down the hill to the blonde girl, fragile, frail, and romantic. And nobody teased or tortured him about it.

You see, love was a part of their lifestyle. Everybody made everybody feel good.

Like the Jewel Tea Company man who'd come to call. He'd prolong his visits there, it seemed to me, talking and laughing at great length, though the mother scarcely bought a bottle of vanilla from him. But he'd leave her plenty of samples before shortcutting beneath the big Potawatomi plum tree as he left. Sometimes the father walked with him a ways with an arm around his shoulder.

In the end, this family seemed better off than most in the neighborhood. Though they were slammed the hardest by financial disaster, they were shining examples because of their love.

The father and mother really loved each other. Next to my parents, they are my earliest recollection of a couple in love, outside of the movies.

I told you about the rocker that was left by the radio in the living room. The man would sit there a lot—though he wasn't an old man—rocking, rocking. Sometimes I'd see the woman sitting on his lap, and they'd be laughing and "loving each other up" as they called it. On such a day I never noticed the emptiness.

When trouble comes, everyone should have a kind of rocker in which to stack up and love away the hurt.

THE SUMMERS OF MY LIFE

Upon those who love, ungenerous time bestows a thousand summers," someone once said. How true that is for me. Sunrise after sunrise over the Wasatch Range. Sunset blending with sunset behind the Oquirrhs and turning the copper Capitol dome into a fiery thing. So many summers the counting is a chore, but with memories enough to have been a thousand.

As summers came and went, each brought its own reward, each requiring something of me. My own marriage pressed young upon me because of war. Then, yet another baby to nurse, another batch of fruit to preserve, another church assignment to fill, another marriage of a beloved child. Until at last, there came one summer's end, a gathering of our family one last time before the youngest would leave for his mission.

We were at the cabin, a little place we had built ourselves in great sacrifice and joy, sharing efforts and sore thumbs with the wonderful larger family of grandparents, uncles, aunts, and cousins as close now as siblings.

We treasured this primitive place where so many summers had been spent so close to stars and wild creatures of the earth and away from the stores and shocks of civilization.

I looked at these I loved and would give my life for—grown-ups themselves now—circling the fire and quietly considering the question their father had put to us, "Well, what have you learned this summer?"

The one preparing for a mission spoke first. "My work at the restaurant put me in company with some people with a lifestyle far different from ours. It's been quite an eye-opener. But then I began noticing how they behaved with rude customers so free with complaints and insults. I learned that 'the soft answer turneth away wrath.' "

The young wife spoke almost with reverence. "I have learned about love. Bryant loves me anyway! And such love makes me want to please him. I'm beginning to understand something about Heavenly Father's ability to love us even when we aren't doing our best."

There had been a recent funeral for a friend of one of our girls, and she had been deeply touched by the fine things said about him at the service. "I thought at the time," she said quietly, "what would they be able to say at my funeral—that I was a good dresser? Bob's death is a dramatic thrust for me to live with more purpose. That's what I've learned this summer."

And so it went, each reporting on books read and discoveries made, of skills sharpened and friendships strengthened, of scriptures memorized and principles reaffirmed, and of the wonder of bearing a child.

"How could the mother of Jesus stand to lose him?" whispered the young mother hugging her firstborn.

It was the summer of my content.

In spite of financial reverses, threatening changes, critical illness, pressures of responsibilities, lost youth, and tender nostalgia, I felt the spilling of my cup as I sat in the circle of my family. This is what living is all about.

My world had broadened beyond the hill on which I grew up, but my heart still found solace in the lessons of those years. Coping is contagious.

From child to grandmother, with my life now matching

the season, I am akin to Albert Camus: "In the midst of winter I finally learned that there was in me an invincible summer."

"I LOVED YOUR FATHER"

I think often of the powerful lessons I learned (and have shared now countless times) from a wine salesman with Italian roots who told me a story while we were airplane-seat companions. He was the youngest of five little children when their mother died. His father was a highly successful wine merchant in the United States. He promptly went back to Italy to find a proper mother for his brood. He fell in love with a schoolteacher, brought her back to the United States, settled her comfortably in the family home, and went on about his demanding business of production and travel. She had two children of her own, and the years passed. At an elaborate celebration for their twenty-fifth wedding anniversary, my traveling companion learned a powerful secret. He said, "I was sitting with our rebellious teenagers and wondering how we were going to survive these years. I looked over at that remarkable woman who had become mother to me when I was a toddler. I wondered how she did what she did. How did she make us all feel loved until we knew no difference between her own children and the rest of us from a different mother? She loved us, and I loved her! I got up and went over to her to tell her so. Then I asked her how she did it—how did she make us all feel so blessedly loved?"

"What did she say?" I quickly asked, my head reeling with remembrance of numerous households struggling with similar problems.

He continued, "She said to me, 'Oh, son, I loved your father, and so I loved his children.' That's the secret!"

He was weeping now as he told me. My own heart leapt to understand that this was the secret to life: we love the Father and then we will love his children.

Always remember and never forget that the human soul is tender and that God considers every one of us worthwhile and precious. So who do we think we are that we can gripe about soiled socks, capless toothpaste, overdrafts, spitting-snuffing-snoring, women with nonstop tongues, and on ad nauseam?

DIRTY SOCKS

Count your blessings if you have a spouse (male or female) who snores! At least you know that he or she is a *presence*.

I comforted a woman following the death of her husband, and she said, "I nagged at him for forty-two years to pick up his dirty socks. He had this habit of kicking them off at night and leaving them by the post on his side of the foot of the bed. When I came back from the funeral I'd have given anything to see those socks in that spot again. You see, suddenly I knew what a blessing soiled socks by a bedpost can be. Even that! They speak of the comfortable, intimate relationship I had with a good spouse."

MEN AND WOMEN, MOTHERS AND FATHERS

---

*To be an extension of Christ in the lives
of his children is the only cause grand enough
for a woman's precious energies.*

"I AM HIS DAUGHTER"

A little boy knocked on the door of my friend's home. He was about three years old—an enchanting age! He had left home secretly, and now he was lost. En route to wherever his little legs took him, he had removed almost all of his clothing. One shoe had been dropped someplace. His shirt dragged off one shoulder. No trousers were to be seen. One stocking was flung over his shoulder, and he was rumpled, dirty, with scraped knees and tear-stained cheeks. He was so frightened that when my friend opened the door and saw him there, she gasped. He burst into tears.

This wonderful lady took the little boy inside and wrapped him in a clean towel while she took his remaining clothing to the washer. She wanted him clean and comfortable when the police responded to her call to find the lad's mother.

In the meantime, she gave him paper and crayons with which to draw a card for his mama. They sang songs and read stories and had cookies and milk. She showed him treasures in her home and read stories from the Bible about when Jesus was a little boy. It was a wonderful time.

Then the police came with "mama," and the little boy started toward the door. He looked at his mother, then looked back at the nice woman who had entertained him so well and said, "Hey, are you Heavenly Father's wife?"

That stopped her. She thought about it for a moment before slowly saying, "No, I am not Heavenly Father's wife, but I am his daughter."

WHAT ARE YOU GOING TO BE?

Children have unusual ways of reminding us of some significant things, haven't they? They can even make grown men think, as I learned one day.

A little boy came clomping down the sidewalk in front of our house in his father's shoes; a tie was looped about his neck, and a man-size belt buckled tightly about his small waist dragged behind him like a tail. A kindly gentleman smiled at the child and asked, "Well, and what are you going to be when you grow up?"

"I'm going to be a daddy," said the boy quickly, flipping the tie. "See?" Then he looked up at the older man and asked the thought-provoking question, "What are you going to be when you grow up?"

The man was startled by such a precocious response, and it caused him to stretch his mind into eternity. After all, that was about the only place he had left to go. And in that context he had to admit to himself that, indeed, he still had some growing to do.

"I'm going to be a father," he solemnly said.

And commitment was born of that comment.

A man doesn't usually dream of becoming a heavenly schoolteacher or a heavenly engineer or a heavenly land developer, let alone a heavenly father. Many hardworking men, if they think about life after death at all, have a comfortable view of a proverbial pink cloud and an eternity of lounging to the music of harpists—or something like that.

Our neighbor knew better than that. The boy's questions reminded that grown man about eternity—about life forever, standing at the head of his own chain of descendants in the presence of God, our Father in Heaven.

Realizing that possibility would make a man think; and it suggests some growing up in a dramatic way, doesn't it? We will need to remember and practice the supreme example of the Savior, who said, "What manner of men ought ye to be? Verily I say unto you, even as I am" (3 Nephi 27:27).

Isn't it interesting that of all the titles of honor and admiration that could be given him, God himself chose to be called simply Father? Since we are in training in life to become like God, our neighbor's answer to the little boy's question was a good one. We are in eternity now, and we are rapidly becoming what we are going to be.

A friend of ours had struggled desperately for years with a drug habit. He had spent time in corrective institutions; his family's resources had been whittled by therapeutic, medical, psychiatric, and legal fees. But he made it. Then one day, when at last he was in the position of graduate student counselor to others who were now where he had been, he was asked by a teenage drug addict how he had won the battle.

"I'd never have made it if my father hadn't helped me," said the counselor.

"Your father helped you? How? My father is part of my problem," the teenager declared.

"Well, he prayed over me like an old-fashioned biblical patriarch," explained the counselor. "He prayed, and he listened to the Lord for guidance. He prayed about 'our course of action' as if we were in it together. He prayed that neither of us would ever give up. He prayed over the professionals—that they would give me the right treatment.

Then he would pray over me that I'd respond to their help, that I'd be able to resist temptation in the tough times, and that I'd be able to hang on and try and try again. And do you know, I well remember the day he laid his hands upon my head and called upon God to bless me and heal me. No, I just couldn't have made it without my father."

How fine a father, how superb a human being is the man who promises that his children in no way will be claimed by the adversary!

One such father spoke sternly to a threatened son, "Son, I'm giving you fair warning. I will never leave your side until you are back in our fold. I will personally pray for you and prepare and tutor you. I will comfort and counsel you. I'll try to be patient and forgiving. But together we'll both grow closer to what God wants each of us to be. Now forgive me, forgive me, my son, for past neglect and lack of understanding that might have brought us both to this tragic moment. What do you say we consider this our time of blessed awakening and get on with our task?"

The father kept his word. These two were subsequently seen everywhere together—on business trips, at the school games, at the gymnasium, at the library, on service projects, and in traditional church meetings. It worked.

Of course it worked. We may recall the thought from the Sermon on the Mount, "What man is there of you, whom if his son ask bread, will he give him a stone?" (Matthew 7:9).

If we care about our children at all and if we stop to think about it, we'd not only give the child bread, we'd give him cake—we'd give him our full love, our full attention.

The question the little boy asked: "What are you going to be when you grow up?" becomes a spiritual guideline for those of us mature enough to be thinking beyond this life's professional pursuits.

A GIRL'S BEST FRIEND

The world is indeed full of remarkable women devoted to being lovingly responsible for other people. Many are anxiously engaged in helping children grow up right. Often women take turns mothering each other; sometimes, even, the tables are turned, and a daughter mothers a mother.

I recall during a serious illness when both the disease

and the medication for it had sorely affected my appearance. One day my daughter and I were walking to a large shopping mall, and I had my arm through hers as she helped me safely up the curb. A reflection on the entrance doors shattered me when I noticed it. I thanked her tenderly for walking with me when I looked so terrible. She gave my arm a firm squeeze and said, "I love you, Mom, and you have walked with me when I haven't been very beautiful either!"

Mothers and mothering can perhaps best be understood in the context of a mother-daughter relationship. A mother, not diamonds as some say, is a girl's best friend.

At work you worry over the family at home.
At home you fret over work left undone.
Behold the working woman's stress.

RECONCILIATION

A young man had been missing from home for three days—he and his motorcycle and his black leather jacket. Where was he? Was he alive or dead? Why hadn't he called home? Yes, he'd been in trouble, but if he'd only come home all would be forgiven. If only . . . if only . . . if only . . .

I was visiting in this affluent home during this time of anguish over a missing teenage son. The parents were professionals, each successful in a field related to medicine. There were tears, prayers, promises, questions, pain, and even accusations as they waited for word from the police department.

At last the doorbell rang, and the mother hurried to answer. A policeman was standing at the door. He informed the mother that her boy had been found and picked up by another police officer. By then the father had come to the door, just in time to see the son alive.

The black leather jacket was ripped. The young man's eyes were swollen, his face puffy, and his hands scratched and scraped. His head was cut. His clothes filthy. It was not a pleasant sight if you were looking for perfection, but if you were looking for a son, he looked wonderful anyway! At least, that's how I felt.

The parents immediately turned into disciplinarians. "Where have you been?" they shouted together at the bedraggled, unhappy boy. Then they piled a barrage of accusative questions upon him. All the worry and caring the parents felt *before* he returned had disappeared.

There was not a word about welcome home or thanks to God. No enveloping arms. No tears of joy.

All we heard was the firm reminder that if that young man was to live in that house he'd have to keep the household rules or there would be worse problems.

Young shoulders sagged. The officer of the law stiffened and turned. A prodigal had been returned, but one wondered how long he'd stay, how much his life would change.

Somebody has to be the peacemaker in such a situation, and it might need to be the parents. Some parents don't realize that they are old enough to know better.

I have come to believe that the story of the prodigal son is the supportive scripture behind the great secrets of personal peace and nightly slumber. It is about reconciliation, which is about Christlike love. The biblical account of the prodigal son is a good bedtime story for grown-ups.

Most of today's prodigals aren't seeking their fortune when they bolt the home fires. They have it so easy at home—what, with comfortable housing, trendy clothing, stacks of sports equipment, and electronic toys ad nauseam.

Freedom is what today's prodigals are after, not the flag-waving kind but the kind that spares their little psyches from the restrictions of family ties that not only bind but also gag, as Erma Bombeck so aptly put it.

Reconciliation becomes a valuable ideal to most parents with such a sleep-stealing problem. After all, they've given the best years of their lives and most of their capital to their offspring.

To me, the most intriguing character in the biblical parable is the father, not the prodigal. The magnificent, forgiving father, the master of reconciliation. What an inspiration! Imagine rushing out to meet that disaffected, selfish, sinning son. And with fatted calf and jewelry, too.

Granted, one doesn't just recall only the father's response. Something needs to be said about the repentant son who must muster the courage to go home and face the music. But it is the father who serves as the example in the scriptural story.

This parable is good bedtime reading for grown-ups largely because of the attitude and actions of the father.

You see, the father did not wait proudly until his wayward son walked in the door, head hanging low as he begged forgiveness. That father didn't stand his "rightful ground" as an authority figure until that son had walked right up to him, groveling and suffering and mortified, expecting a lecture on the theme "I told you so!"

Rather, as soon as the father noted that the prodigal was coming home, though he was yet a great way off, the father ran to meet him. Ran!

There followed a celebration of joy. No doubt about it, family love was stronger than human frailty. Forgiveness was a part of that family's lifestyle. You can be sure both Father and son—to say nothing of Mother—had their first good night's sleep in a long time. The next day is time enough for a rehearsal of rules.

FATHERS AND SUNSHINE

I'm glad you are my dad! What if I didn't have such a great dad?" Cameron said as he positioned the identification tag under the seat of his new bike. The tag read: "Cameron Daley, 2121 Beaverlake Drive, age 7."

Cameron felt his father's big hand steady his smaller one as the tag was secured. At last, his own bike! And the ID tag to prove it. "Dad, I really like my new bike, and hey, you are some kind of awesome." Then Cameron reached to give his dad's arm a squeeze.

Cameron's father smiled. "Good! Now, your bike has your name on it, just as you have my name on you."

"Yeah," responded Cameron absentmindedly as he smoothed his hand over the handlebar.

"Listen, son, take care of you *and* your bike, will you? Believe me, you and your bike had better not show up someplace where you have no business being!"

"Right," Cameron slipped his foot onto the pedal and adjusted his helmet.

"Did you hear me? And keep that helmet on, okay?"

"Okay. Okay! Sure, Dad, I'll keep my helmet on if you will keep your cool. Okay?" Cameron loved his dad, but he wanted to get on with life and bike riding.

"Okay, but remember about the whole armor of God that we talked about last night, got it?"

"Got it!" answered Cameron, already wheeling off with a "grin full of sunshine," as Mom always said. And Dad mumbled to himself, "Proverbs 10:1: 'A wise son maketh a glad father.' "

Almost everybody is glad for you, Dad, whether you think you are awesome or not. It is your caring and your yearning after them—bailing those offspring out of trouble and shifting them into happier ways—that really make a difference in a person's life. You are good for much more than that, too. For example, as a worthy priesthood holder you have the right to preside at special moments involving the laying on of hands—a name and a blessing; the healing blessing; baptism and confirmation; a special blessing before school starts, when assignments loom, or as a mission or marriage get underway. Such blessings can bring comfort and can inspire trust.

How about the aching times on your knees and the sleepless nights when "that boy" defies you as he tries to be a man (like you, Dad)? There may be open battling, yes, but what about the good times when your strong arm, your arm of safety, your kind of affection, your reassuring praise work wonders?

Your love isn't passive, though it may not be demonstrative. Some fathers are famous for playing it aloof, but that isn't true of *all* fathers! There are many ways of taking fatherly responsibility and showing love. There is only one sure way to bring a son into the light of the Lord, and that is by example.

FATHERS I HAVE KNOWN

In these latter days great fathers have trained up great sons, and both have contributed to the kingdom of God on earth in remarkable ways. George F. Richards and his son LeGrand Richards were both Apostles. Joseph F. Smith and his son Joseph Fielding Smith were prophets and Presidents of the Church. Brigham Young was prophet and President of the Church, and his son Brigham Young Jr. was an Apostle. The same was true of Wilford Woodruff and his son Abraham Owen Woodruff.

Because of their relationship, I specifically include here my husband's grandfather George Q. Cannon, who served as an Apostle and as a counselor in the First Presidency, and his son (my husband's father) Sylvester Q. Cannon, who was also an Apostle.

As a family we treasure the wisdom and insight that we found in the private papers of Sylvester Q. Cannon. He was an engineer by profession and a gentle, refined man of God through parental training. Before his mission as a young man, Sylvester traveled with his father, serving as his "secretary" on several trips. That experience provided a sure polishing for him through daily companionship with his father, which included frequent daily prayer, preaching and teaching, blessing the Saints, and sharing the gospel with nonmembers. Sylvester grew up to become the father of seven loyal children and to serve as a mission president, stake president, and Presiding Bishop of the Church for thirteen years. He was ordained an Apostle in

1938, and he served as an Assistant to the Quorum of the Twelve until becoming a member of that body in 1939. His youngest son, my husband, D. J. Cannon, was reared and trained in righteousness and reverence for his forefathers who served the Lord valiantly. To his own posterity, Jim has passed along his own clear wisdom for life and devotion to gospel principles. For example, this quote from Grandfather George Q. Cannon has helped our family over many hurdles: "Though your prayers may not be answered immediately, if they are offered in the name of Jesus and in faith, nothing being left undone by you that is required, they will live on the records of Heaven and in the remembrance of the Lord and yet bear fruit."

With such fathers as we have talked about here, there is a legacy that is most precious and remarkable, really, that can pass from father to son and prove the cultural and spiritual salvation of the generations.

Lynn Bennion has been one of the great educators of our time. His humanitarian style was to give all men their chance in the system. He clearly remembers his inner feelings when he was a young man and his father said a few words that changed his thinking forever.

World War I saw America and Germany as enemies, and the carryover of feelings was difficult to change. An immigrant family from Germany moved into the farm community that was the Bennion family's neighborhood. They were the Buehners, and they were good, hard-working people, but language was a problem, and so they were not readily assimilated into the social structure. This was not a stigma against this particular German family per se. Rather it was a blight of the times against all people from the Old Country. Dr. Bennion remembers well the Sunday morning when his benevolent father put his arm around Lynn and spoke gently but firmly to him and his younger brother, "My sons, go and sit by the Buehner boys in Sunday School. They're lonesome." They did as their father told them. The Buehner boys and the Bennion boys grew up to be prosperous and serving and to be significant leaders among men.

Carl Buehner served as a General Authority of the Church. It was my privilege to be part of his group of Church leaders on a leadership training tour in Europe. In each of the Church areas in Germany, Elder Buehner told a dramatic story of what he had learned from his father. Now a successful American businessman and an important Church leader, Carl Buehner stood before the people of his birth land to describe his first real job in America. It was hard manual labor. Each day he had to haul huge sacks of cement, loading and unloading them to fill orders and replenish storage bins. Each sack of cement was stamped with the company's name and logo—a huge red devil complete with horns and pitchfork! Brother Buehner said his father taught him that when you wrestled with the devil in life, it was hard work to get free of the burden. Carl Buehner grew to hate the devil. "With each bag of cement I lifted and toted I remembered the lesson, and I vowed not to mess with the real devil!" Carl said.

Vaughn Featherstone's sons learned about honoring the priesthood from their dad as he took care to dress in a jacket and tie to perform the comforting priesthood ordinance of a healing blessing for one of them.

Burke Peterson's story of learning from his father about giving his best to the Church is a notable one. He remembers a wonder-filled feeling as he saw his father ironing the paper dollars of the tithes and offerings before he turned them over to a higher authority. He wanted everything to be as neat and orderly and cared for as possible!

One of the abiding blessings of my own life is remembering the way I felt every time I saw my father "crinkle his eyes with tears," as we children called it, when one of us gave some little verse in grade school umpteen years ago or gave a talk in the Tabernacle later on.

Unapologetically, he did this same tender thing as he introduced us to his business friends or to his work staff when we, in Halloween dress-ups, dropped in at his office. The measure of security, well-being, and gladness that a father's evident love can mean to a child is inestimable.

Doug Bagley is a man loved for a lot of reasons. At least one of them is evident in the context of his being a father with a demanding career, one that involves professionally helping others. When we were with him for several hours, taking care of necessary work in his storage area and warehouse, we noticed the relationship between Doug and his six-year-old son, John. This bright-eyed boy followed his dad around in keen interest, not with sulky impatience or shining demands. This boy knew what his father's work was! He was learning it. He learned about interacting with customers, some of them under much stress, as he was introduced to them. He used the speaker system to send messages. He ran errands and followed the instructions his father gave, almost as a matter of course. Clearly this young boy had been at work before. John learned to "work" in ways that stretched the mind, muscles, and scope of the lad. He watched and learned as one who was part of it all, not a spectator. John noted the occasional pat, squeeze, and soda pop from his father. I noted the hero worship in the boy's look. He liked being with his dad in the workplace.

I watched the boy watch the father's warm greeting of the mother when she arrived. Then came the crowning moment for me. As John and his father accompanied me to the door, the boy, looking back to his dad, explained, "He is my *one* father! I am sealed to him. I am *sealed to him*. Mother is my only and always mother." He wasn't just imparting information to me, his newfound friend, rather it was an announcement of the lucky situation he gladly found himself in.

For what more could a child ask?

Smith Shumway is a remarkable man who lost his sight during World War II. He had been well into medical school, training for a career that demanded sharp eyes, among other things. That war injury changed his life forever, but a remarkable attitude and great faith were his help. Now, for more than forty years, Smith has worked miracles with people who have lost their sight. He is quick to credit his father for his inspiring recovery and exemplary attitude of faith. "[My parents] taught me to pray for light and to desire knowledge," he said.

A relative had criticized him with the observation that if Smith had prayed as *her* son had, who was alive and well in a German prison camp, he might not have lost his sight. Smith took the rebuff kindly, remembering that he had prayed and that he was in good company with the outcome—hadn't Jesus himself prayed that the cup would pass from him? For Smith, as for Jesus and a whole parade of faithful fathers and sons through the ages, the attitude of happiness and peace remains: "Not my will, but thine, be done" (Luke 22:42).

It is as the ancient philosopher said (and many have quoted since), "Like father, like son," and as Jesus taught, "Every good tree bringeth forth good fruit." There it is again—that sacred connection between Jesus and sunshine, Dad and sons' shine.

Men are marvelous—just ask them.

MY MOTHER

Mothers do have a way with them. Over the years of living and mothering, I've noticed that my heart is a honeycomb. It is riddled with little cells that close away the vital happenings of my life: small celebrations, disappointment, impossible love, a few innocent pleasures that belong only to the childish days when one sees through the glass darkly.

In the season of my maturity I must live with my honeycomb. I even use this imagery deliberately when I don't feel very brave, locking an emotion in its cell after the fashion of Scarlett, who chose to "think about it tomorrow." Now I frequently seal up grief and death, the giving up and the going on.

Writing about my mother requires that I open the honeycomb, that I think back through to my own spirited earthly guardian: back, back, back to the earliest memory of her—buttoned shoes on a patterned floor as she stooped to retrieve my baby bottle that had somehow jumped from my groping fingers . . . again.

As I write, she is a presence in my consciousness and my affections. She is yet as yardstick for evaluation and behavior.

Oh, Mother dear, I love you so.

Some of you will remember a mother's apron, a special æbleskiver pan, some kitchen skill. My mother cooked, all right, and our house was the scene of food functions of all kinds, including feeding the Depression Era tramps. We carted casseroles to the sick and afflicted, but they weren't "sacred" or "special" as some claim when doing their good deeds. But then cooking was *not* my mother's life, and her red flag of self-esteem. Nonetheless, I learned great food basics from Mother.

I learned to scrape dark toast, turn it upside down, and tap it on the sink edge to release burnt crumbs!

I learned the philosophy of food presentation—almost as important as flavor! We became adept at making radish roses and candlestick salad (you top half a banana with a cherry and poke it into a circle of canned pineapple).

I learned not to serve "naked" food. A bare platter surrounding carved meat, steamed vegetables, or sliced fruit was unthinkable. Dress it with wisps of parsley, mint, or nasturtium leaves. Lettuce, at least!

I learned that paprika was sprinkled "for color" on pears, cottage cheese, deviled eggs, potatoes on the half shell, and baking-powder biscuits smothered with creamed chipped beef.

Some of you will remember a mother's work gloves molded in mud to her cupped hand setting the spring bulbs. Sidonie-Gabrielle Colette wrote of her mother's "radiant garden face, so much more beautiful than her anxious indoor face." I understand that. My mother gardened her worries away, vigorously yanking the June grass from the tangled rock garden out front, pruning the cherry trees marking the back property line, or mulching the floribunda roses. She even wrote a garden column for the *Deseret News* for a time. But my mother was at her radiant best in her book-crammed corner. Here there was an aura about her that was startling. Moving among her variety of books, she became a light herself.

In my mother's study were the workings of her soul—mind-things like reference books, maps, anthologies, a magnifying glass, pencils jammed in a thread box, ruffled pages of mysterious scrawled notes in a lined tablet; tools the body used to enrich the mind and spirit. And whole sets of classic children's literature.

When my mother was mothering, she was so excited whenever she sent one of us to the enormous dictionary to look up a word we didn't know. She would drop whatever she was doing to listen to our findings. Even the beginning readers in our family knew how to use the worn, floppy-covered encyclopedic dictionary purchased from a door-to-door salesman in Depression days. Her eyes would snap and sparkle in a lively discussion with us about usage, too—not only correct English but also the right word in the right place to make meaning exact, lovely, moving.

During first grade I started my own fat scrapbooks,

sitting beside her and pasting in quotes cut from *Pictorial Magazine, Good Housekeeping, Saturday Evening Post, Liberty,* the *Relief Society Magazine,* and the *Improvement Era.* I even laboriously copied mysterious lines I found underlined in her favorite books. Much, much later I came to understand and value the meaning of these things.

Of course, we all grew up cherishing words, ideas, philosophies, phrases, and books—even the feel of the binding, the quality of the paper, and the look of the typeface.

For many years, my own mother was the weekly book review hostess for the Lion House on South Temple. When books were delivered from Deseret Book or when the *New York Times Book Review* section came in the mail, Mother hugged them to her. Selected books became burdened with paper clips, abridging a long book into a one-hour, unforgettable story. My mother was a storyteller. People gathered about her. I once saw a beautiful piece of native sculpture called *The Storyteller.* It was of an American Indian woman with assorted children clustered about. I think of my mother like that. I remember being spellbound by her "book review books," such as *Child of the Sea,* by Elizabeth Goudge; *Keys of the Kingdom,* by A. J. Cronin; *Magnificent Obsession,* by Lloyd C. Douglas; and

Ben Franklin's autobiography. My mother even abridged the biblical history of Paul the Apostle into a near-movie script. All with elastics, paper clips, and margin markings slanted in her swift script.

I don't know what leftover deprivation provoked my mother's devotion to stubby pencils, chewed in her beautiful, flawless teeth, never touched by any dentist. These scarred pencils were regularly yet strangely carved into a new point by a paring knife held against the wood and whittled off in a direction away from Mother's determined body. The shavings fell neatly into the toilet to be flushed away.

In fifty years of keeping my home and desk, I never once have flicked paprika on a pure pear (though I recognize my roots for color consciousness in cooking). I fastidiously avoid chewed stub-pencils. In spite of Mother, or perhaps because of her, I prefer pencils smooth and sleek thanks to a mechanical sharpener and topped with a fresh eraser almost before it's needed.

But, Mother dear, I loved you, so I noticed your ways and rituals all along, though I don't whittle pencil points, I bask yet in all the practical instructions that I received from you—in your ingenuity and resourcefulness. I tenderly remember what you awakened within me. I think about the horizons revealed in the thirst for learning the gospel, the love of words and books and *people*.

A THINKING WOMAN

A thinking woman knows who she is and who she is coming to be. She doesn't spend her time shadow-boxing with gospel fundamentals or sulking over something she doesn't have full information about. God is good, just, caring. He loves women!

And don't let anyone tell you otherwise.

A thinking woman takes her responsibilities seriously, but not her achievements. And she considers her life sacred. She sets goals, seeks blessings, and serves with sensitivity. She forgives herself quickly for not being perfect—yet! Her confidence is in the Lord, and she doesn't flinch—much.

Let us remember that we must move forward steadfastly and with confidence in God in the right direction.

Do you remember that worn but applicable adage that she who hesitates is not only lost but is miles from the next exit? Well, all the more reason to turn to the Lord daily—constantly, repeatedly, as well as humbly, as he has suggested. He said, "Call unto me, and I will answer thee, and shew thee great and mighty things, which thou knowest not" (Jeremiah 33:3). We can be as wise and wonderful as we need to be in life.

There it is again: With God nothing is impossible, and always, always he is there for us.

If it were left to the men to get the Primary talks memorized, shoes found, hair curled, dinner prepared—the family would never get to church. But my husband says it can't be helped—men have to shave every day.

FATHER'S DAY

One of the most impressive reports about fathers was an article describing an effort undertaken in an Indianapolis school district to get fathers interested in their children's school life. It seems the fathers hadn't been supporting the PTA. But there was one teacher in a certain school district who counted a father's influence as so vital to the success of the school child that she determined to find a way to lure fathers into the classroom. Once there, she was sure she could excite them about what their children were doing and convince them of needing their help for greater achievement on the part of their offspring.

She assigned her class members to write an essay, "What I Like About Daddy," and urged them to be specific. A note was sent home announcing the date when these essays would be read out loud in a PTA meeting. It was a meeting the fathers supported.

They came in their small cars, their campers, their super specials. They came in suits and ties, blazers and golf shirts, pullover sweaters and plaid shirts with button-down collars. Some came right off the job in their jump-suits and parkas, slicked up some for the school meeting. They all came reflecting their daily work, their lifestyle, and their personal taste.

They came because they were curious and somewhat apprehensive, too. What would these little children have to say about their fathers?

Now, some interesting things happened when the papers were read. First a random selection had been made from a box full of essays. Letter after letter proved to be quite similar. Each child, according to the assignment, listed what he or she liked about Daddy. Some said he'd built a dollhouse, or helped fatten a pig to sell, or taken them on a trip, or played catch on the lawn out back. But out of 326 letters, the overall thrust was that kids liked their dads because they spent time with them. In all those letters they credited Dad with helping or giving something they needed as being a reason for liking him. Not one of the 326 mentioned what kind of car he drove, how he dressed, where he earned his money, or what size house he'd provided for them. They didn't even describe the way he looked—bald, bearded, tall, or overweight. It was just that Dad was great because he was a friend in some way to his child.

Now, every man came to that meeting with his own opinion of himself and an image of his contribution to his child's life. No doubt there was some guilt felt as he antici- pated his shortcomings and which of them the child would describe before the class. Each went away knowing for certain that he was important to his child in terms of the time he spent doing things with that child. It could be chores or flying kites—but it was time in the company of that father that got written about.

During war years stories of the heroism of soldiers and loyalty to country fill the press. But one of the most touch- ing to me is the story about a lonely spot during the Vietnam crisis where a young chaplain was conducting a worship service for the soldiers. The mix at the meeting was across the ranks—all levels of enlisted men and commissioned officers sat together, seeking strength, worshipping God, their Heavenly Father. Suddenly, as the meeting progressed, it was noted that a broad smile lighted the face of the chaplain. Soon the men saw the reason for that smile. A special guest had come in and walked toward the stand to sit in a chair reserved for him. The plane bringing dignitaries had been delayed, so the meeting had started without them. The interruption was not a surprise; a guest had been expected. Only it was a surprise that the chaplain's father was a last-minute substitute guest for one who had been unable to keep the assignment. Father and son smiled at each other, shook hands, and then embraced each other for long minutes. Many respectful, homesick men wept as they watched. It was as if every son were in the arms of his own father again; such was the vicarious joy of that scene. Some had never had the blessing of such a relationship with their own fathers that would equal the love and companionship exhibited in that tender scene of reunion.

It isn't so much what you had from your father as what kind of father you are that counts. One has some control over that.

Wanting to be a good father and being one aren't exactly the same, but good intentions are helpful. One young man told us of his wonder at becoming a father. He said he fell in love with a beautiful campus queen and married her in fine style. Later, he said, he turned into a father when his wife brought forth their firstborn son. The new father said he felt totally unprepared for the experience of fatherhood, and he winced at the incredible responsibility of it as he beheld the miracle of his offspring. "But I loved him. I do love him," he emphasized brightly, "and I'll love him enough to make up for my unpreparedness. How does a boy prepare to be a father, anyway?"

How, indeed? we might echo. Yet implicit in that sharing is the secret, it seems to me. He loved that baby. If he goes on loving him into manhood, someday a reunion like the one described in Vietnam may take place after years of separation because of school, service for one's country, employment, marriage—or death. Love is the element, and showing it through time spent together was what the children in the Indianapolis school bragged about.

One of the favorite pictures in our family album is the one taken when our son was three years old, wearing his red and blue sweater, sitting with legs swinging free on a chair beside his father's bed, singing him a nursery song to make him better after a serious accident. That picture reminds the whole family now of the hours of devoted care the child showered upon his tall dad during the weeks of recuperation. He did not weary, that little one, of his well-doing. He sang his songs over and over again faithfully. He drew pictures on dad's arm and softly stroked his hair. Books and friends were left aside because his father seemed to need him. Indeed, father purred under such attention. That kind of tender, loving care doesn't happen with sunshine and rain. It comes because a father has loved a little boy enough to win undying affection. A relationship like that has its own reward during later and more trying years.

I think of a young friend of mine whose father was a wheelchair arthritic for all the time my friend grew from a child into a teenager. Neighbors first were worried and then became pleasantly accustomed to the exciting ride to church the boy gave his dad in the wheelchair each week. The son was surefooted and firm gripped. He'd send his father scooting and then run and catch him as they both laughed out loud. Dad had been a ski patrol hero before illness struck. It was a time of special sharing for these two that sweetened the life of both. They loved each other, we all knew, and that's what counted.

One Father's Day program featured family speakers to pay tribute to their fathers. One of the trembling teenagers, with his voice changing and his hands shaking on the papers he held, let the tears flow freely when he looked down at his dad sitting there before him and said: "My father is just like I want him to be. He comes home from work and kisses Mama and lifts the baby up and makes her laugh. He runs his fingers through my little brother's hair and says, 'How's my little man tonight?' Then he puts an arm around me saying, 'I am proud of my big boy. Did things go all right today?'"

The boy stopped after reciting several special incidents that proved his father was a good man. His voice faltered, and he wiped a tear as he finished, "I love my dad. I wish I'd heard him tell me he loved me."

There are many ways to show love, but sometimes we need to say the words. That young man's talk reminds us of that. Let us each express to each other, fathers to sons and back again, parents to children, wives to husbands, "I love you," which translated means, "You're special to me. You make my heart warm. I'm glad we are related."

MOTHER: LOOK AT YOU!

M othering is the best thing to happen to anyone. It is awesome to press a little person's hand in yours with the awareness that his or her life is in your control as well. There swells in you a mix of tenderness and something akin to fear. Prayers come easily in such a mood. Prayers of gratitude for such a privilege as mothering affords.

There is another truth about mothering: when the child is tucked in bed at last—with the hassle of care and cleanup, delay and discipline over for a time—the smile flashed your way makes the effort worth it all. Or a letter comes from your missionary, so joyfully wired now that he gently suggests repentance for the family. And you are satisfied. And instead of wanting to give up, you want to get better at it!

Look at you . . . singing away with the sisters, "Lord, make me a channel of thy peace!" The words may be St. Francis of Assisi's, but they are the focus of a mothering woman's heart.

> *Lord, make me a channel of thy peace*
> *That where there is hatred I may bring love,*

That where there is wrong I may bring the
    spirit of forgiveness,
That where there is discord I may bring
    harmony,
That where there is error I may bring truth,
That where there is doubt I may bring faith,
That where there is despair I may bring
    hope,
That where there are shadows I may bring
    thy light,
That where there is sadness I may bring joy.
Lord, grant that I may seek rather
To comfort—than to be comforted;
To understand—than to be understood;
To love—than to be loved;
For it is by giving that one receives;
It is by self-forgetting that one finds;
It is by forgiving that one is forgiven;
It is by dying that one awakens to eternal
    life.

This is a Mother's Day song, all right, and since mothers are in style every day of every month of the lifetimes under their wing, mothers need such a golden goal. It is an old poem—God inspired, no doubt. It is a familiar song. It is time worn and proven by mothers. It is therefore

83

perfect for a tribute to the absolute oldest and most noble profession and possibility for women.

God has revealed the divinely appointed opportunities for women. No matter how the world carries on—demeaning women, exploiting their beauty and promise, keeping them chattels and slaves, expecting them to single-handedly carry the burdens of parenting in any situation (divorced, widowed, unwed, unequally yoked, working inside and outside the home, supporting a big-deal husband as his hostess as well as wife)—no matter, God gave to woman to be his arm of love. To men God gave his arm of leadership. And God gives no assignment or commandment without providing a way for it to be accomplished. Woman's mothering role, her servant status, can be a blight or a blessing.

But look at you! Carrying on! Counting your blessings, doing your remarkable thing. Remembering that bedtime smile of the loving, needful, grateful child. Conducting family prayers, if need be. Forgiving and loving—even mothering your male family members *anyway! Your* own heart, you see, is warmed and filled by the Holy Spirit.

When we come to understand and obey the gospel of Jesus Christ and the whole exquisite plan of life, we will know that God established the difference in the roles of men and women so that it is not possible for one to be exalted without the other. Some of a mothering woman's divinely appointed opportunities include:

> Becoming a partner with God in mothering his earth children.
>
> Training up a child in the way he or she should go.
>
> Nudging and nurturing a man to goodness and godliness.
>
> Cultivating a woman's unique qualities to discern, intuit, comfort, stand by.
>
> Preparing herself in all ways to fill such a lofty place in the eternal scheme of things.
>
> Seeking wisdom from the scriptures and the prophets.
>
> Seeking learning from the schools of life through books, courses, and people.
>
> Experimenting upon the word of God, which encompasses all truth wherever it is found.
>
> Moving forward, personally progressing as well as enriching and controlling one's life.

Eliza R. Snow said, "Let the women seek for wisdom

instead of power and they will have all the power they have wisdom to exercise."

For me no day in my life can top the day my first baby was brought to me in the hospital—newborn, fresh from heaven, an incredibly lovely miracle. For this I was born. And as each succeeding newborn came, there was a replay of the miracle that lifted my inner heart to its highest. Oh, just imagine the blight on a career lady's life if she were to wake up one morning and remember that she forgot to have children. So much for cramming your life full of nonessentials.

When we do take up the flame of mothering, what is it we are supposed to do, what are we supposed to be like, how shall we nurture? What is it we wish we had as mothers to impart to our children? How we feel about those we mother proves interesting with a closer look. At our house we built up our four daughters, we considered them very special—little princesses. Julian, princess of the Netherlands, on the other hand, proclaimed, "Our child will not be raised in tissue paper! . . . We don't want her to even hear the word *princess*."

People growing up in this, a hostile world, need a very reaching, profound kind of loving and reassurance, steady tenderness, wisdom in guidance even more than knowledge.

Then one day comes the difficult education—the loosening of the ties so carefully put in place in the beginning. For we rear those we mother to move forward, knowing they really won't look back until they are parents themselves and begin to understand.

Consider these remarkable examples of mothering from our sisters in the scriptures:

Eve. He called her Eve because she was the "mother of all living." She was Adam's helpmeet, not just a partner to keep a man from being lonely. As the proper definition of the word reveals, God gave Adam a "helper worthy of him."

Sarah. Now, here is the prime model of faith in God and in his servants. She became a mother after the time of women was done and was the absolute epitome of a noble wife and mother.

Mary. Handmaiden of God. Mother of Jesus. Especially read Luke and Matthew for insights on this inimitable mother. May we never forget her prime example.

Dorcas. She mothered mothers. Her "alms deeds" were so healing that when she died the widows wept for her, and when Peter arrived in her city, he returned her to life.

Sariah. She clearly loved her sons and was concerned for their welfare. Upon their return after obtaining the plates of brass, she rejoiced and bore testimony that the Lord had protected her sons.

It is difficult for a woman to perfect herself in the confusion of today's world. There is an even greater challenge to achieve perfection as we match wits in the relationships that mothering imposes.

But look at you, Mother! Not only are you making it work, but you are also making it wonderful. This is the grandness of mothering. It is the best thing to happen to anyone.

Mother, you are an unforgettable woman. A person who receives a mother's unconditional, unequivocal love knows this. Mothers are so important we simply cannot forget them. What is more, we choose to remember them all the rest of our lives.

We women may talk too much for the comfort of
men, but even then we don't tell half we know.

"THIS IS HOW
I'M SUPPOSED TO BE"

Remember, sisters, a woman doesn't have to stay in the house to be in the home. Neither does a woman need to leave her home to extend her influence to others. We will, however, be more effective on our errand if we have studied the gospel, developed our skills, and reached up and beyond our own first associations. The sooner we start, the sooner we'll soar. Growth is gradual. Time is so swift—crickets call; then Christmas comes. One day a little girl—next day a woman. "Sunrise, sunset," the nostalgic song reminds us. And so it is. Tonight you're twelve, and then suddenly you're in a holding pattern just past forty. There is no time for delay in personal improvement. Proper preparation for life doesn't happen overnight.

I once stood with Sister Camilla Kimball while President Kimball greeted the little children at an area conference. A young mother-to-be rushed toward us and threw her arms around Sister Kimball, hugged her, and wept. Then as she gained her composure she said, "Oh, Sister Kimball, you are so beautiful, so serene, and so supportive to your husband." Fresh tears accompanied this outburst, and then she said, "Oh, Sister Kimball, my husband says this is how I'm supposed to be."

Sister Kimball, who was all that the woman said and more, spoke quietly to her, "It will come. We all have to learn through experience."

The young mother-to-be went away comforted. The beginning wasn't the end! She lifted her head in hope, as I believe we all must do, to move steadily forward in ultimate faith that the end can be better than the beginning, wherever we may start.

WOMEN AS AN INFLUENCE

There are two important days in a woman's life; the day she is born and the day she finds out why. She has just one chance to live on earth—like everybody else. To secure the satisfying life as a bachelor-girl, as a bride, as a grandmother—even as a beginning young woman—she must put into play her every strength, wisdom, wile, talent, and prayer.

We've all heard about the beauty and charm of a bride. There she goes, the misty-eyed bride enveloped in veils of romance, hope, dreams, modesty, allure, and nest building. Her cup runneth over with love. With her hand in the Lord's and her heart in her husband, she moves forward to the adventure of life. And, ideally, one day she will have her hand in her husband's and her heart in the Lord.

This change, of course, is what life is all about.

How does it all happen? What factors make a woman's life what she wants it to be?

A woman whose attitude is mellowed by a closeness to

God, whose life is sweetened by gospel experiences, a woman enlightened by religious training, strengthened by saving ordinances, and directed by inspired leadership, is bound to have a unique view of why she was born. No matter how broad-minded or emancipated, liberated or sophisticated she may claim to be, deep down she knows she is a cherished child of God. She is the recipient, with others of his children both male and female, of all the blessings of a plan of eternal life. The day a woman of any age comes to understand this, to at last be comfortable in God's will for her, is the day she finds out why she was born. It is the day of her own giant step.

The lessons a particular woman has to learn may be different in detail from her sister's. But living to one day claim the fullest of God's promised blessings is every woman's business—or it ought to be.

To learn and grow as a human being is important. To become skilled in one's particular role is the avenue to true fulfillment. Perhaps one of the very good things to come out of the restless women's rights movement over the years has been the intellectual awakening that has come to women themselves. This awakening has been an excuse to consider what it means to be human as well as to be female. For a woman to consider blessings and responsibilities, realities and unchangeables, frameworks and possibilities, is to open a door to fuller living.

Today some women have chosen to enter or been forced into the marketplace, into the mainstream, into the so-called vicissitudes of the hard outside world. Yet if there is to be that precious continuity, the saving sanity, the humanness so necessary to quality life for us all, someone still has to deal with the going to bed, the getting up, the comforting and caring for those with whom we live. It is what women seem especially suited for. It is the reality that the veiled bride must deal with.

It seems unquestionably to be her special stewardship. I personally believe it is her privilege. No matter where her talents, her opportunities, or her situation take her, no matter what her age, really, a woman who cultivates caring about others and influencing them for good is expending her precious energies in a proper way.

In a historical address delivered more than one hundred years ago in New York, Elizabeth Cady Stanton had this to say: "If in marriage either party claims the right to stand supreme, to woman, the mother of the race, belongs the scepter and the crown. Her life is one long sacrifice for man. You tell us that among womankind there is no Moses, Christ or Paul—no Michelangelo, Beethoven,

Shakespeare—no Columbus or Galileo—no Locke or Bacon. Behold those mighty minds so grand, so comprehensive—they themselves are *our* great works! In you center our very life, our hopes, our intensest love. For you we gladly pour out our heart's blood and die, knowing that from our suffering comes forth a new and more glorious resurrection of thought and life."

Well, that is some influence, isn't it? And the bride, trailing her veils behind her, may well be stirred by such perspective.

Great gifts in women often haven't taken the form that brings personal recognition or wealth. Somebody is always needing his hand held, his dinner prepared, her heart comforted, her nose wiped. Some loved one is forever needing a good influence to nudge him through multi-pressured society. And there are only so many hours a day, so much personal energy, and a few citations—Oscars, Tonys, Emmys, or Nobel prizes—given to the girl whose life is marked by selflessness. Maybe that's why the world was so taken when Mother Teresa, so old and worn and yet so unwearying, was presented the coveted Nobel recognition. But awards or not, what rare satisfaction, confirmed by the swelling of the spirit, a person feels when serving God's children in whatever positive way!

For the bride, a younger girl, a woman of maturity, or anyone for that matter, to be a humanitarian and a partner with God in lifting mankind is a noble effort. But to know the fine details of how to implement this ideal in our own lives is something else.

What is the key? It seems to be a matter of quality and goodness, of aliens and fidelity. The June bride and her sisters in any season should look to being what women are especially suited to be, and that is doing great good. To love a child she has never known, to reach beyond the corners of her own selfish interest, to play the supporting role to man, to keep heart in a home, even if she is out of it in the working world—these make a woman of any age womanly.

It is an exciting effort, too, to develop self so we can contribute to others, at last having our heart and our hand in God's.

Never forget the real difference between men
and women. A man comes home from
a trip and tosses his dirty laundry.
A woman comes home from a trip and does it.

DO UNTO OTHERS

And what if God was as we are—
too busy with burdens of his own
to lend a helping hand? Oh, what if . . . ?

ALLIE AND TONY

The earth was ready for winter. Not anticipating it—more like bracing against the fact of it. Flowers had shriveled. Sap had drained to tree roots. Vines had begun to pull free from the walls, some sprays sticking tenaciously like an aged person's frantic grasp at life. Thistle and sunflower pods spattered the lonely fields. Everything seemed shrunken and silent, stark, skeletal, soldiering the season with its onslaught of storms and smothering layers of ice and snow.

It was after autumn's colorful exit, after the teasing frost of early November nights and before nature was used to its own demise. Everything, even the evergreens, was closed up, pinched, packed, laced, locked, and ready for winter.

But sometimes the waiting went on. Sometimes the season never came to its full.

Like Allie.

Allie was a hopelessly crippled arthritic who seemed forever destined to be alone, cushioned in her big chair, pounding walnuts open with a rock on a breadboard. She couldn't grip another kind of tool, so she hammered and pried her days away, awkwardly flicking the nutmeat free with a flat-handled ice pick.

And that was Allie's life—winter-wracked.

Until we moved in next door.

Allie lived with her sister in a bungalow surrounded by hundreds of tulips that had been left in the ground so long they had reverted to basic yellow. The quiet the sisters had known before we became neighbors disappeared when six children and a dog promptly made a path through the tulips, the hyacinths, the phlox, and the petunias in turn of bloom. And that first year, waiting for winter, we trampled the stems and stubble as well going to their door. Next spring there would be a proper path built but meanwhile, no complaints, just a warm welcome.

We all loved visiting them, but it was Tony who really eased Allie's pitiful brace against winter. And Allie accomplished the miracle of proving how early a child can learn all manner of marvelous things if he is taught from the beginning in patience and love.

It all began the day the heavens finally released their load upon the waiting world. Snow, the great common denominator, equalized everything white. When the storm stopped and there were no more snowflakes to watch out the window, the children made frantic preparations to get outside. The bundling began. Leggins. Mittens. Mufflers. Caps. Sweaters under coats. Dad's old socks over shoes and under galoshes. One slips a child into a waterproof zip suit these days, but then it was a long process to find winter swaddlings for six.

Meanwhile, Tony, our toddler, well under two, couldn't wait for his turn at the dressing. I felt a cold draft from the open door before I missed him. His tiny footprints in the snow, with a stumble or two clearly visible, marched right to Allie. I followed the trail and the scramble marks up the steps to the door. There through the front window I could see them already at play. Her head bent to meet his as she pointed out letters, taught him simple songs, explained life.

I was grateful to find him bundled against the wet and cold, but we had to agree upon some ground rules.

No one must be imposed upon. Allie's strength must be preserved. Tony's mother must know of his whereabouts. His schedule had to be protected. But even these faltered finally in the face of Allie's need and Tony's hunger to learn.

Some said, "Don't you care that he wants to be there with her so much?" (Rather than with you, they implied.)

Care? I wondered at the question. How can we be so blessed? was a more accurate reading of my feelings. There was no way I could have given him that kind of attention just then. My life was so pressured and energy so spent. Five children in a row had come along almost as fast as they could. Then finally, some time later, Tony came, the second son we had been promised. This child was special because of circumstances too sacred to relate here, and I did not want the ordinary demands of motherhood to deprive him of the personal attention he ought to have.

Allie was an answer to my prayers.

What her body lacked in mobility, her mind made up for in creativity. Little "people" were torn from bits of paper. Moistened with a finger on the tongue, they came alive to ride a pipe-cleaner horse, perform on a box stage, sail in a walnut shell, star in a game of letters. All the while, principles were being taught about goodness and greatness, giving but sharing, too.

Allie was a bountiful benefit to Tony. In time she bloomed like the apple tree in our orchard, signaling that winter was finally done with.

As he grew he brought her things from his world outside—a spider in a glass jar captured at fall's edge; snowflakes on a pie tin hurried inside before they could melt; a bird's egg fallen from the horse chestnut tree; rocks scrubbed and ready for her to choose a favorite from; and endless "writings" he had scribbled at home.

One day Allie made a grammatical error that Tony corrected in a comfortable way each had become used to.

"That bird's egg looks lovely speckled like that, don't it?"

"Donuts are what you eat," was his reply. Then he picked up the egg to check the speckles while she smiled.

The heart knows no barriers, suffers no generation gap. So they grew together these two, through the winters when a child was bored at home and Allie was trapped in her cushions. He awaited the storms and the times inside with Allie. And when spring came he would often sit with her on the porch in the evening while the stars were counted and the moths were explained and his wonder in the world increased.

Then early one spring, quite suddenly, while Tony was still young, Allie died in her sleep. Her winter was over. We wept with the rain that this precious chapter was finished. Weeping endures only for the night, and joy does come in the morning, for Tony's life had been influenced and Allie's heart had known love.

She spoke gently. Tony does, too.

Sometimes when the snowstorm is heavy with soft flakes that cover the ground quickly, I think of Allie all those long years ago and the mothering she and I shared.

And I thank God for her.

It is easy to thank God for this friend and for other friends, for adventures, awakenings, and miracles.

THE MAGIC OF COOKIE-CUTTER SANDWICHES

The daffodils Nedra Warner had poked into a bean pot were for the centerpiece of a movable feast that our son and his sons were to enjoy. His wife had just passed away, leaving three little boys below kindergarten age with their dad. Nedra had come to help the afflicted.

"Life can't be a picnic every day," she announced when the door opened and the four faced her, their frozen hearts matching the snowy day behind her. "But today you are going to have one!"

The mood changed when this rare and lovely neighbor swept in with a picnic basket crammed with all manner of delightful fixings. And the daffodils. The children quickly caught the spirit and helped spread the checked cloth in the center of the living room floor. As a centerpiece, toddler Jared plunked himself down with the pot of daffodils, and the party was on.

What a departure—a picnic in the living room with Dad nodding approval! Nedra hadn't brought a casserole—not for a parlor picnic. She packed food fit for fussy children.

Cookie cutters had turned sandwiches into intriguing shapes—animals, angels, and stars. The names of the children were printed with cheese squeezed from a tube on the top of each sandwich. The carrot and celery strips were skinny slivers that a child could chew. Everything was prepared with the little ones in mind. Wisely, she let them discover the treats without the bustling about of the typical do-gooder. Nedra brought her movable feast, her condolences, and left the bereaved family to enjoy their feast in privacy, all happier for her efforts.

MY NEIGHBOR! MY FRIEND!

The young mother was a real beauty, very chic and trendy, in excellent taste. Her fingernails were salon enhanced. Her shoulder-length hair had been highlighted, and it caught the sun's glow like a halo as beams streamed through the church window. Her knife-pleated skirt flipped enchantingly about her shapely legs, snugly encased in black tights. She finished her Relief Society lesson with a sweet prayer, and the president, Marge, who was not so chic nor so young, stepped quickly to the teacher's side, and they embraced, warmly patting each other's shoulder in the tender exchange of love. "Trudy is my neighbor! My friend!" said the president to the women gathered there, before announcing the closing song and prayer. Trudy's eyes filled with tears, and her chin quivered as Marge paid tribute to her.

For six weeks in the coldest, snowiest part of the season, Trudy had gathered up her new baby, her toddler, and her eleven-year-old and braved the elements to do kindly deeds for her friend and neighbor Marge. In disguise as the Relief Society president, Marge actually was the most needful of the sisters. She was a widow. She had undergone back surgery and was having a tough recovery. She lived in a split-level house with steps and stairs and couldn't navigate for a time. All her high-school-age children worked after school to help with the family finances. But Trudy was there to start the washer, fold clothes from the dryer, collect the mail, vacuum, and accomplish some personal grooming for Marge. Others had been assigned to bring in meals, but Trudy brought in heart and hope in such a way that Marge—remembering—counted her as a blessing.

THE KINDNESS OF STRANGERS

I had ridden to the airport in Manila, Philippines, with my husband, who was on his way home. Because of typhoon warnings, it was doubtful whether he'd be able to take off. My driver and I watched the plane lift into the air just before the airport closed. By the time I was safely in my room on the twenty-second floor of the Manila Peninsula Hotel, the typhoon was raging like nothing I had ever experienced before, and I was frightened. The power was out. The palm trees were horizontal in the flooding streets. When it was too dark to see anymore, except for flashes of lightning, I climbed into bed. I had never, ever felt more alone. I literally pledged my hand into God's and reverted to my childhood prayer-poem, "Now I lay me down to sleep, I pray thee, Lord, my soul to keep. If I should die before I wake, I pray thee, Lord, my soul to take."

In the morning, destruction was everywhere, and no sunshine. My top feeling was gratitude that I was alive and that the elevator was working so I could make it down to the lobby. I was in a sensitive, sober mood as I waited to keep an appointment with my driver to take me to the war memorial of the casualties of the Pacific theater, World War II. He was late but was willing to drive me to the sacred, deeply impressive place. It was my first time there, so though it was pouring rain, I wandered alone beneath the tall arches so I could scan panel after panel of thousands of names for the names of my friends who had fallen in the line of duty. There were many, of course, because it was, after all, *our* war. Then I found the name of a boy I had known well since childhood. Long years ago I had danced with him to the big bands, exchanged little gifts, and indulged in long phone calls. When I found his name I was surprised at my reaction. Suddenly my tears were a match for the weather. I was not prepared for the enveloping of the Spirit I felt at that moment. I lifted my face to the weeping wind and gave in to solemn grief. Yet I felt gratitude in the memories. In spite of the turn life had taken, we had had one wonderful time as lighthearted youth.

My driver had been watching me and came to my rescue with an enormous black umbrella. He'd seen others go through this experience. He was a fine, typically poverty-stricken Filipino who lived with his wife and several children in a community where the pitiful homes were made of packing boxes used in shipping. The typhoon had flattened their home. Crude as it had been, it was all that they had had. My driver explained this and said it was the reason he was late for our appointment that morning. He had been helping to unload new packing boxes delivered to the site so people could rebuild their shelters. And I realized he'd taken time off from that work just to indulge some American lady!

Joy came in suddenly understanding God's statement regarding the worth of souls and in recognizing the quality of God's children and the contributions strangers make to strangers whether in war or heartbreak.

A LOT OF GOOD
PEOPLE OUT THERE

Frequently we are reminded of unpleasant things that people are doing in the world. The media spread the stories daily. But we know there are a lot of good people out there who are making a good difference to the quality of life.

There are a lot of good people out there who are doing common things in an uncommon way and making this world a nicer place to be. Anne Morrow Lindbergh wrote, "My life cannot implement in action the demands of all the people to whom my heart responds." We understand that dilemma, yet it is heartening to see many people quietly doing good in spite of their own pressures. Here's one example:

A family had put everything on the line to help their father during a bitter political campaign. He lost. Six children close together in age had worked long and hard. They were new to this kind of disappointment and took the defeat painfully. With defeat went hope of financial recovery as well, because few people want to pay the political debts of the loser.

The day after the voting, the family gathered glumly about the table, trying to bolster each other's spirits during dinner. A neighbor knocked at the door and followed the mother back to the dining room. Rather than accept their invitation to sit with them, he stood at one end of the room and began talking to them. He wasn't someone they'd been particularly close to. His business was in Detroit, and he seldom was home; but he knew something about heartbreak and dashed dreams. He told the family about the need for people to help make our communities better places for families to live. He praised the father as one who was willing to get into the thick of things when others—including himself—couldn't or wouldn't.

Then he asked them all to look squarely at their father while a special presentation was made to him. The visitor handed the tearful man a lovely ceramic figurine of a soldier, and he said: "This isn't Napoleon; it's just one of his troops. Without the troops, however, there would be few heroes. Never forget the value of one man's willingness to work for the good of others. Never forget your own efforts as part of a team in public service. You may feel financially down at the moment, but your father has given you more than money can buy. He's given you a wonderful example."

That thoughtful neighbor put a father back on a pedestal before his children.

I heard about a group of teenagers in a city neighborhood

who organized what they call The Terrific Taxi Team. They sign up for duty and put themselves on call for senior citizens who don't drive anymore but have places they need to go just the same. These youth happily drive the older people to doctor appointments, to the drug store, to a friend's house, to the shopping mall, or along the countryside just for the joy of it. They don't always wait to be called, either. They telephone their clientele and ask if there is any place they can drive them that day. Isn't that great?

Here's another example of neighborly goodness.

Carl is the kind of person who is a blessing to a neighborhood. He makes everybody feel good. The countless kindnesses chalked up to his credit are something to shout about, only Carl won't do any shouting. He figures if people need help, somebody ought to help them. And that somebody is often Carl. Some years ago a family whose baby girl suffered from a congenital hip defect moved into his area. She was placed in a body cast and could only lie flat, either on her back or her stomach. She was miserable most of the time and so was everyone else in the family.

One night after Carl had been visiting them, he stayed up very late trying to figure out something that would allow the tiny child to sit upright while the bone healing took place. Finally, some time later, he was successful. He had rigged a kind of bicycle seat at high-chair level that had special sidebars to hold the child securely. Carl's caring changed the family's life. Other families in this kind of difficulty wanted an orthochair, too. And Carl obliged. The design was patented later, and now many people have been helped.

Some people ask how they can help, but others just go and do it. In Reno I met a blind girl who was graduating with honors from the university. It hadn't been easy, but she wouldn't have earned her degree at all if there hadn't been good people out there helping. As a freshman she was full of hope that she could do it on her own, but campus life wasn't designed for her kind of problem. One day she stood in the registrar's line waiting to withdraw from school. She passed the time visiting with a stranger she couldn't see.

The problem was shared and a solution was found. The stranger gave hope and counsel to our blind friend. She was not to withdraw from school. She was going to be helped. The new friend would organize some of her Lambda Delta Sigma sorority sisters into shifts of service. They'd take her to class; they'd help her with notes and monitor her projects. That's exactly what they did for four years. When graduation time arrived, the applause for the blind girl was most enthusiastic from all those who had invested their caring into her success. After the ceremony there was a sweet weeping and warm embracing. Oh, what a difference good people can make!

When our children were small, I had serious surgery that proved a trial for a time to our family. Being laid low at the height of the fruit harvest was a frustrating spot for a mother of many to be in. It was worse because we lived in the middle of a small orchard, and my bedroom window framed a peach tree burdened with its ripe fruit. Only I couldn't get to it. My husband was out of town on a business emergency, and our helper at home had her hands full with all the little ones. I needed those peaches; and I recall crying silently while I prayed for peace in the face of this waste.

It was while I slept under heavy medication that Bea came to our property and picked the peaches. The next day she returned with nearly sixty quarts of fruit fit, to my marveling eyes, for the state fair exhibit. Only another woman knows the work behind sixty quarts of bottled fruit. Our family ate them with a special kind of reverence all that winter. Well, Bea saw the need and did the deed, and I will love her until I die.

How can we really thank those people who invest their humanity in others? There are no songs of praise sung for them, no news stories today, no name in lights nor a bronze plaque in the hall of fame. Maybe we can pass on only our thanks, as the saying goes, by doing good for someone else ourselves.

Eliza R. Snow, a gifted poetess of the Western pioneer movement, sat with a group of friends for a kind of celebration of compassionate service one to another. This wise woman said, "Let us all watch over each other, that we may sit down in heaven together."

That is a particularly motivating thought for those of us who are determined to do better in making a difference in life, as so many good people out there are doing.

WHAT GIFT
FOR YOU, MY FRIEND?

Two pushing-past-middle-age gentlemen friends had a reunion at a social gathering lately. Living in different states now, they were glad to be together informally. Arms around each other, smiles wide, eyes alight with remembrance of very choice times in the past—ball teams, missions, singing groups, and courting days.

"What can I do for you?" one asked the other. "What can I give you?"

"Sing!" someone interrupted. "Sing your duet." And they did, hesitant and feeling each other's pace at first but suddenly bursting forth in good voice and close harmony their theme song from other days, "Two Boys from Utah." And the onlookers were mellowed, softened in their own remembering of friendships while enjoying the awareness that good relationships last, no matter the distance in time and miles and the demanding public responsibilities that burden successful people.

Coworker, neighbor, sister, brother, tennis partner, child, spouse, doctor, church worker . . . *friend,* because the elements were right when circumstances brought togetherness. Association ripened the relationship.

Time makes friendship valuable—time filled with countless small favors, efforts, demands, and moments of being there. Chemistry, too, of course. Friends, however, need not have all that much in common, except each other.

And with such a friend, so long enjoyed, the fact of gratitude swells into action sometimes. What to give such a friend—in thanks, in love, in a gesture to brighten a life, lighten a load, or simply underscore value in a relationship—

like flowers blooming better with cultivation and care, so a friendship that is nurtured now and then seems sweeter.

What can we give a friend?

A song, yes. Some old sheet music found in a house move. A hymnal with a favorite message marked. A duplicate tool for her son's first home. A first violet of the season. The last rose of summer. A volunteer Potawatomi plum tree with its young roots balled for easy transplant and a jar of new jelly to sell the deal. Mint and rosemary for her herb garden. A cassette of mood music. News clippings proving that the goodness of people still exists. A quote suitable for her presentation at literary club or church.

Taxi service.

Pastry when her children are coming to visit.

Pastry even when they're not!

Red peppers from the garden and chili sauce from the pot.

Strong back, ready hands when there is crash cleanup needed.

Lemonade delivered on a hot day. Steamy spiced cider on a cold one.

A bouquet—even if it is cut from a garden catalogue—when she's honored for birth or accomplishment. A new scent for self-esteem, such as lavender in a lotion or gardenia in a bar soap.

A scriptural passage relevant to a current need. One that is inspiring any time. Another that points a certain way. One that reminds and comforts. Still another that underscores hope. Etcetera! Each written out and sent daily for prolonged support.

A bank, for a paperweight or for quarter saving, but proof that you bank on her, that she can bank on you.

That's it . . . any small thing that underscores a choice relationship full of trust, humor, support, and availability whenever.

THE MAN FROM THE TAVERN

When our family was young, the eight of us were crowded in a two-door car on a Sunday afternoon (yes, it was a car that was too small and too old, but in those days we were fortunate to have a car at all). We had been to a missionary farewell in a suburb off the north-south freeway. We'd barely entered the on-ramp when the car choked and sputtered and stopped.

We were hot. The baby was crying. Everybody was

hungry and needed to get home fast. We watched people empty the church down the road that we had just attended, climb into their cars, and drive right on by us. No one stopped, even though the children waved and called out of the open windows and my tall husband stood hopefully beside the car with its hood up. We were very disappointed and surprised. We watched. We prayed earnestly. Finally help came from a tavern across the freeway from the church. A man leaving the tavern drove up on the on-ramp, saw our plight, and backed up on the shoulder to rescue us. Frankly, he was quite overcome with our enthusiastic response to his help of pushing us to the nearest gas station. We couldn't get over him, and he couldn't get over us! We have talked many times over the years about the irony of those churchgoers—supposedly true believers in the example and teachings of their Lord Jesus—compared with the man from the bar.

GOD BLESS THE
SICK AND AFFLICTED

Across the pulpits, beside the beds, around the tables at mealtime, from the kneeling circles of families beginning a day, in holy temples, in busy hospitals, and in private places, countless good people offer the universal plea at prayer time, "O God, bless the sick and afflicted."

What a comforting thought that is, because sooner or later we all qualify to be counted among the sick and the afflicted. How good it is then, to be included in somebody's prayer!

Afflicted is an interesting word to describe a terrible state of being. Suffering an affliction brings miserable images to mind, such as boils, shingles, bankruptcy, terminal disease, miserable personal relationships, heartbreak, death, deprivation, succumbing to temptation, or being struck down by disaster through no fault of our own.

Dictionary definitions of "affliction" include such designations as torture, suffering, persistent anguish, torment that strains the powers of endurance or of self-control, extreme embarrassment, and stress of mind and body from whatever demanding cause.

Mercy!

When you are among the sick and afflicted, you probably are plagued with accompanying feelings of doubt, hopelessness, and self-pity. You need to be reassured that you are of some value, and that life is worth living. You hang on the promise that all this experience will, indeed, be for your good. You want to feel sure that God lives and cares about you, particularly at this time.

Until this current sickness or affliction is resolved or has run its course, you seek comfort, patience, strength to endure, and sustaining support. You want God's blessings. While you may know the sweet uses of adversity when it is your turn to be among the poor, the sick, or the afflicted, prayers are a powerful force in helping you get through the siege.

There are countless choice reports of the miracles wrought in healing, of resolution and peace resulting from God's goodness as united prayers from the faithful pour out before heaven.

Regarding those prayers for the sick and afflicted, there are some people who when they pray, "O God, bless the sick and afflicted" include a request that they themselves may be directed by heaven to appropriately bring comfort or cure to others in their times of assaulting affliction.

What a refreshing idea!

Doing something for others is still the best way to forget your own troubles. That's when joy can come.

God bless the sick and afflicted?

He does!

HELEN WINGET

In Fillmore, Utah, near the center of the town there was a fast-food place that featured home cooking. For many years Helen Winget not only served up the best hamburgers and shakes between Salt Lake City and St. George, Utah, but she was a friend to many in need. The kind word, the listening ear, the generous deed, the quick answers to a traveler's questions, a bright smile, and a gentle word—all were on her menu as she greeted the public. In recent years this attractive woman moved a mobile home next to the little cafe. There her father-in-law and her husband, both in very poor physical condition, would rest where she could keep close watch on them and still earn their livelihood serving the public.

The amazing strength, personal discipline, and faith of this woman carried over as she dealt with others. Only a few suspected the load she carried. They noted only her compassion.

Several years ago we stopped for refreshment at Wingets'. We learned of the passing of both men from a waitress. Then the young woman said, "Oh, Sister Cannon, let me get Mrs. Winget. She'll want to see you."

In a few moments Mrs. Winget appeared, seeming to

be vastly different. She was desperately unhappy, lonely, and feeling unneeded now that her charges were deceased. Change brings its own assault on our emotions and stability. It was a different kind of affliction she was suffering that day.

Mrs. Winget and I embraced a moment and then she said, "I need someone's arms around me. I need someone to care about me today—someone who can understand from experience what I have been through. God brought you here today!"

It was her birthday, I learned from the waitress. We surprised her by leading the patrons of the hamburger stand in a rousing rendition of "Happy Birthday," complete with a lighted match stuck into a fudge sundae and a small speech in tribute to a great lady because of the years of friendly helping.

"I NEEDED TO DO A GOOD DEED"

There comes a time when your heart is broken, your spirit is sagging, your feeling of self-worth is thin. You admit there is reason enough for such depression in this current set of circumstances. You deserve to be somewhat unstrung, even devastated. But you learned long ago that fruitless crying delays resolution to problems, and life is about problems. Therefore, it is good you've learned how to work through them, isn't it? So score one for you!

You check out your emotional symptoms to discover why you were weeping instead of being someone who stifles grief or hurt by dutifully doing one's duty no matter what milk is spilled. Whatever the details behind this particular trauma, the fact is that you are feeling blue because you are dwelling on the dark night with its disappointments. Instead, look to morning, when joy cometh; thanks be to God who made the sun to rise as well as to set.

When you turn to the Lord in need and in increasing faith, the comfort always comes. It has never proven otherwise. That is the thing to remember. And when he has helped you, you quickly turn to help others.

A lovely lady named Linda came by to see me one frazzled, dumpy day. She had a pumpkin pie in hand.

"What have I done to deserve this?" I happily asked.

"I don't know, really. I needed to do a good deed, to live outside myself in love. Your name came to mind. Maybe I was inspired—who knows? Anyway, don't thank me, thank the Lord. But if the pie isn't good you can blame me!"

"What do you mean, you *needed* to do a good deed?"

"I woke up burdened with my grief. I'm just not used to being a widow yet, I guess, and I turned to the Lord, of course. You'd think he'd get so sick of me. Well, a few precious minutes of communion with God and I realized that though my husband wasn't resurrected at that moment, I wasn't alone. I had a few debts to pay, that's all, and so I needed to do a good deed."

And you know, that can be true with any of us. Maybe we need to do more good deeds to find ourselves "girded with gladness."

THE GOODNESS
OF MAN AND OF GOD

Jesus said he knows his sheep, his followers. And in time of personal struggle it is lifting and helpful to remember that he knows you! And as you reach to know him, you can hear and feel his caring comfort.

How do you hear Jesus?

Recall the account given in 1 Kings 19:11–12, which

says, "And, behold, the Lord passed by, and a great and strong wind rent the mountains, and brake in pieces the rocks before the Lord; but the Lord was not in the wind: and after the wind an earthquake; but the Lord was not in the earthquake: and after the earthquake a fire; but the Lord was not in the fire: and after the fire a still small voice."

A suggestion to the struggler longing to hear Jesus is to come to know that he is and that he cares. You don't look for him in the big noise of the forces of nature. You listen deep within your soul for a still, small voice. Then you can know (*know!*) that he is talking to you, mindful of you, aware and concerned about your special problems and needs, as differentiated from what others are going through at the moment.

Let me share a sacred-to-me experience to underscore this idea. During a dreadful snowstorm pelting us on a mountain highway, the wonder of God's goodness to an individual in a given moment came home to my heart again.

My husband sat in the passenger's seat, the victim of a paralyzing stroke, and I was driving under perilous conditions. Suddenly our car went into a spin and slid off the freeway shoulder and down a slope into a ditch. I tried to move the car, but it was embedded.

I got out into the storm and surveyed our situation. Fortunately neither the car nor we were hurt. However, the deep, wet, freezing, fresh snow quickly covered me, the car, and our tracks. There was no way to get the car moved back to the freeway without a wrecker. There was no way I could help my husband up that hill into the line of traffic, where we might pick up a ride. Understandably, no one stopped to offer aid in that treacherous situation. The snowplow hadn't widened or scraped the roads yet. The time stretched long, and the storm assaulted the scene. I was beginning to feel desperate. Then a thought occurred to me.

We were in the deep ditch—but not out of touch.

We had prayed for protection formally, as is our custom, before starting the trip that day. We prayed again as we sat buried in our car. And at last, one more time I got out of the car to tie a red bandanna on the antenna and alert the cars going by, trusting that someone would report our plight to the highway patrol. It seemed almost hopeless though, and I was frightened and frustrated. We had prayed! My husband was quite helpless in this setting. I was a mere woman! He had a relative who, some years ago, had frozen to death when their car stalled in a mountain pass while his wife went for help. This thought plagued my mind, and all calmness left me. I started to kick at the thick, encrusted ice over the headlights and radiator grill. I was angry. Then suddenly I cried out loud. Oh, I was contrite now, and desperate. I was brokenhearted and helpless in a way only God could ease, under the circumstances. My anguish and full faith in God pushed through the falling snow, "Please, don't let him freeze to death here and now."

Naturally, I was sobbing. I turned to walk back toward the driver's seat and the miracle we needed happened, that fast. The Good Shepherd had heard my voice! A huge, four-wheel drive truck had stopped. The driver and I struggled to get my six-foot-six husband out of our car and up the treacherous snowbank. It was an impossible situation.

And then in an amazing act of bravery (under the circumstances) as well as goodness, the driver of a passenger car risked stopping to pull up behind the truck. A big, strong stranger came forth and bodily got my husband up the slope and into the truck cab, disappearing as quickly as he had come. The truck driver proved to be a fine former bishop who took us the remaining two hours right to our home door.

How does a person ever repay such kindness? We are, as King Benjamin said, forever in debt to God. And to man as well. This was a frightening experience for us, but because of God's blessings it turned out well, and we learned all over again the goodness of people as well as the goodness of God.

WINTER COMES
WHEN THE HEART BREAKS

Winter comes in life not by solstice, not even by the first snowfall. Winter comes when the heart breaks, regardless of the season. And often the heart breaks because of what we do to each other.

It begins early in life when choosing up sides for a game. For example, nobody should be chosen last every time! When everybody else gets chosen for a side when you are playing teams in baseball and you join a side simply because you are the last one left, it is not good. It's terrible. Humiliation. Rejection. Heartbreak.

Winter.

And that's what happened to me for one whole school year.

It was the time of depression in the land. Girls wore hand-me-down dresses of cotton print—sash tied, puff sleeved, and hemmed to meet our cotton socks at the knees. Our sashes were forever being torn loose, and the socks seldom stayed put. Baseball was our life, and dresses were poor attire for it. But so it was.

Two baseball diamonds had been made in a lot adjoining the school—one for boys and one for girls. Whenever the ground was somewhat dry during the year, we played baseball at recess, baseball at lunch, and baseball after classes. It was because of Maude and Virginia. They loved baseball. They were sisters and the most incredibly good baseball players you could imagine. We all worshipped at their feet and declared them undisputed captains of the two teams.

Maude was older and could pitch "faster than sight." Why, half the hitters missed half her throws most of the time! She was smart as a mynah bird, and cagey. She had been sick a time back and had had to repeat a year of school, the way they did then, so this put the sisters in the same grade, two grades ahead of me.

Virginia was bigger. She could catch a fly without a

mitt. She could bat that ball, then lope around home before the out team rallied to act past their shoutings. She threw the ball like a boy.

So their teams pretty well balanced, no matter how the rest of us got portioned out. Each time we played, the opening ceremony was repeated. We would choose up sides for teams, with Maude and Virginia "eagle-clawing" the bat to determine who got first choice and therefore who chose last.

After a while I realized there were never going to be any surprises in this for me. I was left until last every time. Out of all the regulars who raced to the playing field, I was always chosen last. Maybe it was an understood fact, but that didn't help my hurt. Our baseball game was one of those times in life when enthusiasm didn't make up for skill. After a while it wasn't who was chosen when that interested me, it was which of the sisters would have last choice, because that made all the difference to me.

If Maude eagle-clawed the bat, that meant she got first choice, and Virginia got me. Which was just fine, because she would pass off this crisis to her team with, "Oh well, I can hit hard enough for both of us," and beckoned me after her.

Somehow that inclusive statement comforted me.

If Virginia eagle-clawed the bat, Maude was left with me. And that's where the trauma came in. Virginia would choose her last team member and then, inevitably, Maude would turn and walk out to the playing field, as if I didn't exist. Not a sign! Not a beckon or an instruction! Not a comment or even a complaint! Nothing. As if I didn't exist.

Whenever things turned out this way, I would shiver, even if the fall's last warmth still hung over the school grounds. But I never threw up, which was some kind of personal victory, because a sensitive nine-year-old with a digestive system like mine could stand only so much social shivering.

There was a period when Virginia had a run of winnings at eagle claws, and I was about to give up baseball and be rid of the anguish of Maude's silent treatment of me. But one day I read something in the *Women's Home Companion* while baby-sitting that gave me renewed hope. "Don't let your passions spoil your dreams," a youth writer counseled. I don't think it had anything to do with baseball, but baseball was my dream right then. My mortification over when I was chosen had to be kept under control if any dreams of making it on the diamond with the other girls were to come true.

So I kept on going to the field, but now I had primed myself for the test. Positive action was to replace negative reaction.

First, I parted my hair down the middle and abandoned my barrette. Though the effect with my long narrow face wasn't necessarily an improvement, it was a change. I hoped it would be an attention-getter. The outcome of that effort, however, did little for my situation. Nobody noticed.

Next, I studied my facial expressions—grimacing, smiling, squinting, and sweetening in front of the bathroom mirror. For hours I concluded that a lift to my eyebrows would make me look more alive, more capable at play. Maybe then I'd be selected earlier in the lineup. I couldn't stand the tweezers, but I had seen one of the roomers at my friend's house use a straightedge to clean off her stray hair. So I took Dad's razor and stroked my brow. In one sweep the entire half of my left eyebrow disappeared, which wasn't what I had in mind. There was nothing to do but match the other side to it.

It never matched, of course, but I had to stop trying or I'd be left without even a dot over my eye! I tried marking the eyebrows back into being by using a burnt match, but people kept wiping "soot" off my face, and I was left until last anyway.

Next I spread graham crackers with pink powdered sugar frosting, folded them in Wonder Bread wax wrappings, and hid them in my coat pockets to produce at eagle-claw time. Bribery didn't work either. They ate my cookies, those captains, while choosing up sides, leaving me until last. Every time.

Though the chill winds blew through me, I didn't give up. I took to praying on the spot, urgently crying out in my soul, "Please don't let me be last. Please let one of them choose me sooner." But if my prayers reached heaven, the signals weren't heard by Maude or Virginia.

Finally, I took to silently rooting that my "enemy" Maude would win at eagle claw so Virginia could choose last. Then I wouldn't have to suffer the humiliation of being ignored by Maude at the end of the choosing. This shifted my concern from me to something else clear through that season. That was good.

That's how I learned to face life's winter, a storm as it came, not a season in full, with "self" at the bottom of the list of concerns.

The traumas of childhood often mark the beginning of the stamina for certain suffering in maturity. I have always believed that there is a very grown-up spirit inside the infant body. The kind of thing that hurts in childhood can hurt in maturity. The ramifications may not be so sweeping, and understanding self-control can change things, but the roots are the same.

Maybe that's how I understood about Gerrard and could comfort his folks some when the need arose.

When they found Gerrard dead "by his own hand" at sixteen, people exclaimed foolishly, "Why would he do such a thing? Why?"

Why, indeed. The answer is implicit in the question. That's exactly why Gerrard did a thing like that. Nobody knew enough about him deep inside to even arouse suspicions along the way. It was done and over, that tragedy, with people still wondering why.

Perhaps it was Gerrard's way of ditching the winter in his life. Winter, all day, every season, year after year. And heartbreak.

He was left until last at choosing time. Nobody rooted for him when they fenced at the church on activity night or wrestled at the gym. Nobody mopped the blood off his nose when the customary after-school fight finally stopped.

And nobody ever invited him to a birthday party.

Over the years Gerrard had grown fat and fluffy from fast foods stuffed in to while away the lonely hours. He ate lunch alone in the cafeteria, wandered solo through shopping malls on Saturdays, and had the top row to himself at all the games.

Maybe people tried.

Maybe Gerrard tried.

But it wasn't enough.

The problem seemed to be that Gerrard had never known about "caring." He was a foster child who had been taken in, hopefully at last, by a small-town childless older couple. They were unequipped for the abrasive patterns of personal insecurity from childhood hurts that Gerrard had developed. The foster parents gave him room and board, clothes and equipment, an allowance for treats and good times with his friends. But there were no friends. They didn't know how to help him with that. And they didn't know how to give of themselves.

Gerrard gave people nothing except the occasion for the question of "Why?" at his suicide.

Oh, why do we do what we do to each other?

Dachau, one of those infamous Nazi concentration camps of hell for Jews, has been turned into a kind of memorial to remind people what people have done to each other. There is a sign there that sobers the visitor: "Man cannot trust himself in the hands of men." The evidence seems obvious at Dachau.

I have read about concentration camps and have recoiled with my generation in disbelief at the hearings after World War II. Being there was deep agony for me. My mind, my heart, the very core of me, was overwhelmingly bruised by my personal Dachau experience.

I went curious, of course, but somewhat hesitant, too, and at the insistence of a dear friend who felt everyone should see this place so mankind would never forget. And I will never forget.

Doggedly we began the charted course through sparse exhibits and pitiful pictures of the devastation—of emaciated, tortured children of God. Hundreds and thousands of them, their souls staring out through cavernous eyes.

I couldn't really look at the pictures. It was much like people walk by a coffin at a viewing, only glancing toward the deceased unless they are halted by a family member who asks, "Doesn't she look lovely?" Then it is the more painful to look, and you wish you'd done it on your own.

Once at Dachau I looked at a picture closely at my companion's invitation. Life sprang from the flat photograph of people who had suffered even beyond desperation. My heart constricted with cold, deep and biting, like being chosen last as a child.

It was overwhelming to me. I somehow felt implicated.

("Forgive me," I silently prayed. "Oh, forgive me, Lord. I was growing up. I was way out in Utah when all of this happened. But forgive me for silence, for not understanding, for not caring enough for so long.")

We pressed forward through each phase of the complex in mounting horror—on through barnlike barracks with wall-to-wall, ceiling-to-floor bunks; on to community rest-room facilities; on, then, to those sinister bathhouses where gas jetted through "shower heads" to kill the numberless masses; on finally, depressingly, incredibly, out past open trenches like the ones where the dead had been dumped and plowed under.

Unprepared for the impact of this place, I wanted to cry out in a long overdue wail loud enough and long enough for the dead to hear—the killed and the killers to hear and know. For all mankind and God in his heaven to hear and to know.

But no cry came. The ache was too deep, the awful awareness of man's evil ability to hurt man was too constricting for anything but silence.

They say the sun never shines over Dachau, so dark

were the deeds of those days. It is true my own tears fell unnoticed, so wet were the skies while we were there, and I thought of the old French saying, "Il pleut dans mon coeur comme il pleut sur la ville" (It rains in my heart as it rains in the city).

One goes home to teach the children never to kill anything, even a fly. And never to break a heart.

What puts winter in one person's heart may pass as only a temperature drop in another's. Fears of the unknown, physical injury, some kind of deprivation, haven't contributed to my stormy times. People have and still can. People always have affected me deeply one way or the other, chilling or warming my sensitive soul either by their suffering or their joy, or mine.

Once I met a successful businessman who smiled slowly when our introductions were over.

"You don't remember me," he said.

"I'm sorry. No. Should I?" I regretted the oversight, however innocent.

"No problem. We were depression kids when our paths crossed before. I was poor folks from the shack at the top of the long wooden steps where the hill slopes into town. Remember the place?"

I remembered.

"I lived there all during my high school years and didn't have a friend in the world. No one would even dance with me. One winter's night at a church function I mustered my nerve to ask you to dance. I knew I was in over my head, your being one of the 'in' crowd and all, but I decided to go for broke."

"What happened?" I ventured.

"We danced! Not only that, but you were nice to me. Maybe this sounds crazy, but it's true. That day hope came back into my life. How could I ever forget you?"

("Oh, forgive us, Lord, for man's inhumanity to man in all the small ways, too!")

Winter comes not by the solstice but when the heart breaks. When our tranquility is threatened, our loved one lost, our dream dashed, our regrets engulfing, and whatever else, a pall comes upon us. It is endurable only finally when Christ becomes part of our being. If we did to others as he did, the tide or error in man's relationships with man would soon be stemmed. Christ is our model. He asked forgiveness for those who crucified him. He gave the sop of friendship to his betrayer and took the basin to wash the dust and pride from the feet of his servants and disciples. He spoke of casting the first stone, of beams and motes, and of how to treat prodigals. He blessed the unclean and comforted the mourner. He defended Mary before the bustling efficiency of Martha. He labeled loving others as the great commandment and warned that because of iniquity the love of many would "wax cold."

To keep our own love from waxing cold, we can strive to be more like him. We can be a light and not a judge, caring about others enough to save reputations, protecting the innocent, sparing heartbreak by what we do or do not to each other.

It is indeed a wintry day when we live as if Jesus had never lived, as if he had never died, as if we had never once been touched by him and his spirit of love.

A CHRISTMAS EVE GIFT

Life is increasingly better when it is based on adherence to higher gospel principles. Blessings flow to a family as, gradually by precept and example, they learn to live by the first and great commandment and the significant second one, which is like unto the first. It is about loving and testifying of Christ in thought and deed and loving Heavenly Father's other children with as high esteem as he holds us. It is about respectful, kind behavior toward each other.

The following family event illustrates my point. It was the morning of Christmas Eve, and I took a phone message for our high school son who was working. The caller was a young man asking if Tony could work for him that night, Christmas Eve. They were busboys at a very fine local restaurant.

When Tony came home, I passed the message along.

He balked. Christmas was his favorite time.

I mentioned true Christmas spirit.

Enough already. He had just finished working and was exhausted. I was ruining his day.

I urged that it would be a nice gift to give someone in need.

He flatly refused and went to his room.

(The trouble with today's housing is that everyone has "a room" to hide in. Surely rearing children was easier when everyone mixed in the hogan, the tent, the igloo, the pioneer cabin, or the tract house.)

Actually, I didn't want Tony to miss the Christmas Eve family gathering either, but the other boy had a very good excuse for needing a substitute. Besides, this seemed an opportunity to discover the true meaning of Christmas.

Also, I knew there would be times ahead in Tony's life when personal sacrifice would *have* to be made whether it was Christmas Eve or not. Learning how to function in a life of service to others seemed better learned sooner than later, since a mission call awaited him in another year or so.

I consulted the scriptures. Bearing one another's burdens is part of the covenant of baptism. It was God's idea and not mine; this was not just a family bylaw. God clearly supports that "do unto others as you would have them do unto you" is a golden rule of human relationships and happiness. I went to his room, knocked, and walked right in, Bible in hand. Tony was resting on his bed with his back to the door. Touching him gently on the shoulder, I said his name in love, for I did love this youngest son. He grunted, which was a clue that he was alert enough to hear the beautiful lines on love which I read from Matthew 22:39: "Thou shalt love thy neighbor as thyself." I asked, "What do you think? We could juggle dinner and the program so you could also help your neighbor, so to speak."

Grunt, groan.

"Does that mean you want me to call him back and strike a deal for a split shift? One works early and the other takes the late shift, you know, do unto others. Then each of you could pick up some of the Christmas spirit. Okay?"

"Okay. Okay. O-KAY!"

Still, he did not roll over to look me in the eye. But I turned the stereo volume up so that "Oh, Come, All Ye Faithful" resounded into his room. He did go back to work, and he came home later liking himself (and me) better.

LOVE

Being loved is flattering.
An exchange—where love is received,
and also returned—is God's gift.

IN HEAVEN WITH YOU

Love at its best, God-blessed and satisfying, is about heaven. At this point it is heaven on earth, to be sure, but it is all we know of heaven, yet.

There once was a perky three-year-old, wise beyond her years and charming already, too. She's grown now into the lovely lady her beginnings promised. What makes her memorable is something that happened when she was three and living in London with her parents.

Following a big meeting of people who love the Lord, she stood beside a woman who had just given a talk. To the little girl it must have seemed like a long talk, but as the crowd pressed about the woman, a veritable stranger to the child, the little one reached to tug at the lady's skirt. It caught the woman's attention, and she looked down into a face, small and radiant, full of innocence and love. The child's eyes held the woman's as she in her small voice said, "I love you. I want to be in heaven with you."

And the speaker knew that in that sentence was the sermon she wished she'd given.

People of all kinds—of various age, color, temperament,

station, and pursuit in life, but of purity and acceptance, too—loving other people . . . how good it can be!

Love loves anyway. The best love is expressed when people put their hands in God's and do helpful service to others in his name. They live so close to Jesus that the Holy Spirit spills over and bathes and washes and enriches and heals those they serve.

Remember the woman who touched the hem of the Savior's robe? She had been ill for many years and had spent all that time with many physicians in an effort to stop the "issue of blood," but it had become worse. She had heard of Jesus and said to herself, "If I may touch but his clothes, I shall be whole" (Mark 5:28). She pushed through the crowd from behind Jesus to secretly touch his robe.

Jesus sensed the woman's presence. While other people merely pressed about him, she *connected* in faith. And Jesus healed her, saying, "Thy faith hath made thee whole; go in peace, and be whole of thy plague" (Mark 5:34).

We who are trying to be like Jesus, who have taken upon us his name, his work, and his ways can reach out in need to others and receive their healing love and help. We can give love and help to those who touch our lives.

Of such is the kingdom of heaven.

AT BAPTISM

O Father, I have promised thee
To humbly take His name,
To love Thy children, do His will,
And thus choice blessings claim.
Be swift, my soul, to love, to serve,
To do His work today,
To meet the needs with fitting deeds
Of lambs who've gone astray.
O Father, let me serve Thy Son
To move His kingdom forth,
To praise His name, and why He came;
To help men know their worth.
Be swift, my soul, to heed Christ's call
To love and feed His sheep.
I'll pray, be still, and learn His will
And thus my promise keep.

HEAVEN'S FIRE

A life in which love has surfaced is sweeter, more sanctified, and more satisfying. Exhilaration mingles with sacrifice and produces winged joy!

Love has been called "heaven's fire." It is like the sun

shining over the whole earth—through love everything is seen in its best beauty. With love dictating the gentle, wondrous responses to God, nature, and all mankind, life has an awesome luster. It is amazing to realize that even unrequited love quickens the mind and flows back to soften the heart. True love ennobles.

But the withholding of love because of grief, envy, fatigue, self-pity, anger, lust, or sin is a mighty loss in life. It is to live as if Christ never lived and died for us. It is to deny ourselves the opportunity of drawing near enough to him to bask in His lifting Spirit, to be inspired by His example, to be touched by His compassion.

"Bridle all your passions," Alma counseled his son Shiblon, "that ye may be filled with love" (Alma 38:12). There it is. When we have allowed our hearts to focus on negative emotions and self-defeating anxieties, we have no room for the workings of the Spirit. Only love and worship of Heavenly Father and Jesus Christ open our souls to the healing and peace that love bring. God is love, you see. The emotional upheaval of the adversary is not.

To love is to be closer to Christ—to match in our actions and thoughts the most profound and refining ideals of Deity. It is to be awakened to a pulsing compassion, a compelling awareness of all mankind. Finally, it is to feel the very real, grand expansion of the heart that spills into laughter, kindness, hope, and unending gratitude.

Lovers aren't perfect people. However, love can flourish in the wake of each other's efforts toward pleasing one another. The worth of each soul is great before God and should be of great value to lovers who covenant with God to cleave to each other and none else before God.

FILLED WITH DIVINE LOVE

Our experiences in mortal probation seem to be very much connected with our effectiveness in communication. Communication with God is essential to our eternal life. Communication with our fellowmen is essential in building satisfying relationships. Even the message of the Restoration itself centers on communication between God and man. Missionaries are communicators of this vital message.

As communicators, we must remember that communication—the process of sharing information, feelings, interests, and mutual concerns in order to develop empathy and understanding—depends on establishing relationships of love, trust, and respect. Between God and man, these relationships are developed by sacrifice, obedience, and faith. Just as sin keeps us from eternal life, failure to communicate keeps us from enjoying the fellowship of both God (see Ether 2:14) and man. The consequences of poor communication are devastating: lack of understanding, deterioration of lives and relationships, failures of goals and plans, and growth of negative feelings.

The positive effects of good communication, however, are great. Through such communication, we bless each other with words of encouragement and testimony. Good communication is a sign and principle of love. It depends upon our forgetting self-interest, personal ego, and the need to be right; it depends upon developing Christlike love. Christlike love will give us an honest desire to understand another person's perceptions, emotions, and real underlying message. We may check our understanding by making clarifying statements or asking questions. We should listen carefully and ask for feedback. Understanding may not bring agreement, but it will improve relationships. Also, blaming never solves a problem; often we ourselves need to change and repent. Seek first to understand, then to be understood.

When we are filled with divine love, we will be positive in our demeanor, attitude, and speech, and we will radiate the Spirit in both word and action. We will consider each person's level of faith, understanding, concerns, needs, and interests. We will establish the proper atmosphere by resolving concerns, expressing love, praying for him or her, praying in the right spirit, and taking time to communicate our true intent. We will be candid and honest yet sensitive to the needs of the situation and the individual. Our goal will be to leave the other person feeling better for having visited with us.

When difficulties arise, we will remain humble (without blaming others), focus on the problem, analyze the situation, and generate possible solutions, broadening the options instead of looking for a single solution. We can stay open to solutions by asking "why" or "why not" instead of taking an immovable position. We will treat solving the problem as a mutual concern and look for mutual gain in the solution, involving others in the decision where appropriate. When we ourselves need help, we will entreat others with love, be grateful for assistance, and express our need in a way that will bring about empathy and a desire to help.

Finally, we need to communicate honestly with ourselves through meditation, pondering, and self-evaluation. Total honesty is important. We must recognize our divine potential as well as our need to make changes, including the "mighty change," by repenting with a broken heart and a contrite spirit (see Alma 5:14). If we will purify ourselves and exercise great faith, God will give us powerful language, as he gave Enoch (see Moses 7:13), Nephi, and the brother of Jared (see Ether 12:24–25), and the power of the Spirit will carry our message to the hearts of men (see 2 Nephi 33:1).

Christ promised that if a person will love him and will keep his words, the Father will love that person, and together the Father and the Son will come unto that person, and, he said, 'make our abode with him'. There is the essence of love.

We begin with basics, with serving. We continue in good works, in loving as Christ loved. We end as companions with God.

152

WALK IN LOVE

To take another look at love through the scriptures broadens our perspective as it narrows our resolve to be more like Jesus. For it was he who walked in love, who washed the feet—who removed the sandals and washed the dusty feet—of his close associates! He gently permitted people to love him in whatever way they were capable of at a given moment—Martha, Mary, Magdalene, John, Joseph of Arimathea.

We understand that man's expression of love should go toward God first and toward our fellow human beings. When we show forth love toward God with all our heart, might, mind, and strength and in the name of Jesus Christ serve him by loving and teaching and helping others, we will be filled with God's love. We will be changed.

We become anxiously interested in helping others feel and know what we feel and know. We are conscious of all God has done for us in the smallest ways, which escaped our attention and thanksgiving before. We are repentant—we want to be what we need to be in order to make heaven on earth and to qualify to be with our Father in the next life.

It is our goal to follow the admonition in Ephesians 5:1–2 to be "followers of God, as dear children; and walk in love."

"SHE NEEDS YOU TO LOVE HER"

Christmas was trying to come into one extended-care center where my mother was a patient. The halls were swagged with kindergarten-like chains made in a therapy class by people with stricken bodies. Bows, bits of holly, and other adornments of the season were stuck to the pin-up boards by each room door. Christmas cards from loved ones who still remembered were taped above the hospital beds.

I came bearing a small tree and a shepherd set for my mother. Mother was in her ninetieth year and bedridden. Her brilliant mind was worn through and she had settled for events of the moment and not too many of those, either. Her condition was difficult; but on this day I learned an important truth: Mother's choice spirit was intact. True, it seemed buried beneath the burden of deterioration of the flesh, but it was eternal!

LOVE

It had been more than a week since I had been in town and I was trying to make up for it. I put the tree on the hospital table and arranged the shepherd and his lambs at the base, chirping along about this and that to Mother while I worked. I got no response from her. Not even the business of Christmas roused her. She was lost in her own vague world.

Overcome with the pity of it all, I cradled Mother in my arms, feeling like a child again, even though now I did the enveloping instead of Mother. Once you lose your mother you also lose this option, and it was only a short time later that my mother died.

Suddenly our tender moment was rudely interrupted. One of the "wanderers" from a room down the hall turned in through Mother's door and came to the bed where I crouched, holding mother in my arms.

The visitor crowded against us and flailed her arm between us. It was a jarring intrusion. I reacted accordingly, straightening up and staring in disbelief.

"Hug her! She needs you to love her," Mother slowly explained, gently pleading with me.

Mother's world was the nursing home now and narrow indeed. But her innate goodness was evident. She couldn't call me by my name, but she could still command my behavior. I did as she instructed, my heart swelling. Inside that poor body Mother lived! Seen or not, Christ lived and influenced!

Love is a verb. It can be a quiet feeling in the heart, but the best love is shared and shown. Both the loved one and the one loving benefit from the joy that happens when something wonderful is done out of love—for one particular loved one or for the human race. Love should be considered an action word, with people moving out to spread joy in today's world.

Bear each other's burdens, the gospel teaches, and we come to love God more. We learn that his principles, given to us to live our lives by, work. They really work!

LOVE ALL PEOPLE

God loves all people. He expects us to do the same. Our goal is to try to become more like him. We begin by keeping his commandments, gradually improving our ability to do so. We start with a single act and move forward as a way of life.

Suddenly there is no more contention in the land—the heart, the home, the neighborhood, the city, the nation, the world.

Is there a precedent for this?

Yes. The city of Enoch was so committed to Christ that the whole city was finally taken into heaven!

Yes, again. In the Book of Mormon we learn that for two hundred years after the Savior had taught and blessed the people on the American continent there was no contention in the land because the love of God was in their hearts: "There were no envyings, nor strifes, nor tumults, nor whoredoms, nor lyings, nor murders, nor any manner of lasciviousness; and surely there could not be a happier people among all the people who had been created by the hand of God. . . . And how blessed were they! For the Lord did bless them in all their doings" (4 Nephi 1:16, 18).

Among the blessings they enjoyed was the healing of the sick. In the name of Jesus Christ the disciples healed the sick, raised the dead, and caused the lame to walk and the blind to see.

People may not be perfect, and surely none go through life without trials, but it is attitude and behavior, the ways of coping and helping, that make the difference. When people esteem others as themselves they are quick to reach and lift and praise and rejoice in another's success and weep over another's heartbreak. When the heart isn't locked up in self-centeredness, it is open to God's influence and sweetening Spirit. It is then that war—caused by anger, contention, jealously, and greed—is crowded out. On every level there is peace.

The outcome of this attitude is families who not only exchange hugs, loving kindness, and patience but also never give up on each other. From family to friends and neighbors ripples the ever-widening circle of good influence.

For abiding in love, first try to apply gospel principles, get over the problems, straighten the ways, and love each other as God's children. No matter what the minute configurations are, we all are part of the grand family of God!

And the family of God abides in love.

Love not only lasts, it is contagious.

HONEYCOMB

Have you ever seen a wax honeycomb taken by a bee-keeper out of a hive? Each cell is sealed off from the others and filled with its particular treasure. It is a thing of natural beauty.

The heart is a honeycomb to someone who has lived deeply. The various experiences of life—the hurts and joys alike—are sealed off from each other. Only then can survival and flourishing in personal growth happen.

How full of proverbial honey are the honeycombed hearts of people who love people and life! These are they who live richly, who are attuned to life's possibilities, who are sensitive to others—responsive to particular people in a particular way. These are they who are open to the feelings of gladness and sadness that inevitably come when one invests in life by taking risks, leaping in faith, caring more about others than self. These are they who have loved and lost and who have loved again by making adjustments in self, by dreaming another dream.

The idea of a honeycombed heart seems apropos to the kind of life we must learn to live here on earth. Seal up the experience that is over, and get on with life.

But there is more. Understanding the nature of life, we

should remember to cherish each other in the recognition that we do not know how long we shall have each other— or how long we'll have a certain pleasurable assignment, or a certain association.

ISN'T LOVING WONDERFUL?

Adam got his name because he was the firstborn in his family. His father was excited about this new baby he and his wife were expecting. I went to the hospital for the delivery because our daughter-in-law's parents were serving a mission and couldn't be there. A new mother likes support at a time like this!

Our son stood by her side to assist with the miracle of the birthing. I waited just outside the door. Just seconds after the first sound of the new baby's cry, the door flew open, and the proud father burst out to announce to me, "It's a boy. Mom, it's a boy! And I just love him!"

Have you ever seen a brand new, just-born baby? It is *not* the most gorgeous thing in the world. It is a squiggly, squawking, suffering, sticky, red-skinned little creature with matted hair (if there is any hair!). Arms and legs wave and kick, contract and thrust. It is an amazing miniature of humanity.

And our son said he *loved* his newborn.

I knew how he felt—how all parents feel at such a moment. He'd hardly had time to check over his new baby or see it cleaned up from the birth process. He surely hadn't had time to build up any kind of relationship with him, but he loved him already. Awesome! You see, the baby was something—someone—he had helped to create.

"Isn't it wonderful, this loving?" I asked him. Then I went on to say, "Do you know that this is exactly the way I feel about you?"

"It is?" The new father was surprised. His mother loved him the way he loved that new child in there? How could that be? He looked at me somewhat embarrassed because he wasn't feeling for me what he was feeling for his newborn; and here I was, his mother, proclaiming love for him, *my* child.

"Yes, I love you as you love your firstborn. But let me remind you that when Adam is grown and a father, he probably won't feel much different toward you than you do toward me now. My reward is that you love your children as I love you. God loves us more than we love him, too."

We talked for a moment about the miracle of birth and the growth of love. "Though it may be hard to believe at this moment," I said to him, "you will love all your children as much as this one. Our capacity to love our children cannot begin to compare with Heavenly Father's. Now that you have a child, you have a little idea of how Heavenly Father loves you, his spiritual offspring. One day you will learn to love Heavenly Father as your Adam will learn to love you."

Love is a seesaw. Love does not stay the same, but is always the most important endeavor of your life. One of you is weak where the other is strong. Each waits upon the other while progressing toward perfection. That's the ebb and flow of relationships built on true love.

PEACEABLE THINGS

Even the phrase "peaceable things" settles one's mind right down. For a moment the angry hassle of the institutional world disappears in the consideration of peace and love and contentment.

Blue-sky talk, you say? Ah, but God says it is possible. And through God all things *are possible*—love in place of loneliness, fulfillment in place of frustration, peace in place of turmoil.

Regardless of the world—regardless, even, of others in a room—there can be peaceable things in your life!

Such an idea comes by good authority—the word of God. We learn in Doctrine and Covenants 39:6 that the Holy Ghost *teaches* the peaceable things of the kingdom. Love is one of the peaceable things. Such a coveted condition! One cultivates the companionship of the Holy Ghost, heeds its promptings, and thus draws from this source guidance and power to improve personal relationships in life.

All right! But there is more . . .

It is startling to come across a scripture like the one that concludes section 130 of the Doctrine and Covenants. This verse declares that a person may receive the Holy Ghost, and it may descend upon that person, and yet not tarry. What is implied here is the doctrine with which we each should be familiar—that the Holy Ghost is able to function (to teach, comfort, warn, enhance, witness, and so on) only in an element of purity and faith.

The Spirit prompts us to do a loving act, a particular

good. Our prayers for guidance put us into a position to follow through. Proving helpful to our perspective are the examples among ancient prophets in the long history of mankind. There is good material to live by in the book of Ezekiel, and on this subject of love, particularly verses 31 and 32 of Ezekiel 33 are pertinent: "And they come unto thee as the people cometh, and they sit before thee as my people, and they hear thy words, but they will not do them: for with their mouth they shew much love, but their heart goeth after their covetousness. And, lo, thou art unto them as a very lovely song of one that hath a pleasant voice, and can play well on an instrument: for they hear thy words, but they do them not."

May we strive to become more pure and full of faith; may we be wise and not only hear the word of God but also do it, that we may know love and the peaceable things.

FRIENDS AND ENEMIES

We hear a song, and our heart melts. We think of someone well loved so long ago. The feeling is still there! It surfaces by a chance hearing of melody!

LOVE

A scent in the air makes our breath catch . . . can it be? No, just the scent on a stranger or a free sample in the cosmetic department as we walk on by. Yet for us that fragrance is tied to a person we used to love—love still, apparently even though the relationship is over.

Quite by chance one day we read something like the following lines from Rupert Brooke: "And the hawthorn hedge puts forth its buds, / And my heart puts forth its pain." We relish the agony of remembered love. Pain is a part of loving, but making enemies never should be. For love remembered is still its own wonderful reward.

There are in the world so many worthwhile people to care about, to like and enjoy, to find affinity with, even to put on your prayer list—to love with Godlike love, so to speak, without aching of passion.

For a moment, see the faces, say the names in your mind.

The favorite teacher, the beloved departed baby-sitter, the hearty and helpful storekeeper, the counselor we visited in time of trouble, the neighbor who welcomed someone else's pets and children and endured trampled flower beds, the personal friend we've loved since childhood.

These were choice people . . . easy to love.

But how about—shall we say it?—the not-so-choice

ones with obnoxious personality traits? Can they be loved?

Can we love the mechanic (or whomever) who cheated us?

Can we love the absolutely tiresome acquaintance who demands so much attention; who, when a smile is given, assumes intimacy exists between us; who demands time, energy, a listening ear?

Can we go on loving the child who is defiant regarding family standards; who is in constant trouble with school authorities and the law; who is obviously in deep trouble and is a plague on parental energy? Can we?

We aren't talking just about God's commandment to love all men, here; we're talking making life more pleasant for ourselves as well as others. Why be miserable in relationships when we can look for something to appreciate, to love about someone else?

Fact: We want to be forgiven for our shortcomings— carelessness, being overweight, thoughtlessness, bossiness and busyness, judging, and so on. We want to be loved, appreciated, regarded highly, recognized (call it what you will).

The Savior's word: "And as ye would that men should do to you, do ye also to them likewise. For if ye love them which love you, what thank have ye? for sinners also love those that love them" (Luke 6:31–32).

These are great lines. But wait a minute. Now we're not only to love the cheating mechanic; we're also to love our enemies—the person who spreads false rumors, keeps us out of Rotary, poisons our pets! We're not only to love our fellowmen; we're also supposed to look at the broad picture and find something admirable, acceptable—well, tolerable—about "the mechanic" or whomever. Life is too short to have unpleasant relationships. It is too long for hating.

Conclusion: We are supposed to be better than sinners.

We are supposed to polish our good points, eliminate the questionable traits in ourselves, and ever move toward perfection, exaltation, and forever happiness. God's rules and his will are for our good. What can be good about loving our enemy? He ceases to be an enemy, that's what! He ceases to cause the soul to sour, at least.

We can learn to love our enemies by heeding the all-important counsel and secret of success given to us by our Creator. "I say unto you which hear, Love your enemies, do good to them which hate you, bless them that curse you, and pray for them which despitefully use you" (Luke 6:27–28).

This is our charge. And though an enemy, an angry family member, a disgruntled repairman—or, on the grander scale, a nation—may disregard our teachings or scoff at our friendly efforts, it is still our commission to love our enemies and other unpleasant people about us.

Each of us can show Godlike love to our enemies by being "an example of the believers," as Paul declared to Timothy. Paul went on to give instruction about how to do this. He said that one should be an example "in word, in conversation, in charity, in spirit, in faith, in purity" (1 Timothy 4:12).

What a giant step forward toward peace, even heaven on earth! What a boost in our personal progress toward becoming even as Christ is!

A GRATEFUL HEART

Whatever our personal burden or cross to bear might be, we are here. We live! We learn! The Grand Adventure is under way for us. Terrible as our trials might be, we are blessed and not abandoned by God.

THE GIFT OF TROUBLE

There is a framed saying in my office that reads: "There is no such thing as a problem without a gift in its hands."

I keep that quote there to remind myself and the people I counsel with that good can come from trouble; blessings are an outgrowth of trials well met; trauma enlivens the heart; clouds have silver linings; and the leaf will burst again on the dry branch.

I once interviewed a remarkable old gentleman who had been confined to a wheelchair since his youth. This was before the time of ramps and parking privileges for the handicapped, or even driving and household equipment that aided the paraplegic. Society largely looked upon anyone who was stricken as different, as an oddity to be avoided—the old gentleman knew all about that. In addition, he had lost his wife and family, and he struggled to keep himself going. His livelihood wasn't courtesy of United States government welfare handouts, either.

It was rougher then than it is today.

"You have had trouble all your life," I said to him. "How have you faced it?"

"Young woman, I don't know what to reply to such a question. I have had nothing but blessings all the days of my life." He smiled warmly.

"But you are in a wheelchair," I insisted. "It is obvious that you have had bad luck. Yet you regard this as a blessing?"

"Why, yes," was his quick and firm reply. "I've been lifted around by some of the best people in the world, and they'd never have paid me a bit of attention otherwise."

He was thoughtful a moment, and then he said, "I do remember, however, the day I decided that since I'd never lift anybody in and out of a wheelchair, I would have to do my lifting in my visits with them."

Then came the memorable line, "I have learned that what God said to Abram of old was true for me, too. 'Fear not, Abram: I am thy shield, and thy exceeding great reward' " (Genesis 15:1).

Surely that's true of us, too.

Robert Louis Stevenson has long been a favorite author of mine. My mother read me pleasantly to sleep with *The Child's Garden of Verses* and then introduced me to *Treasure Island*. I have recently come to understand what the man really went through to produce his fascinating tales for posterity to enjoy. He recorded in his journal the following: "For fourteen years I have not had a day of real health. I have wakened sick and gone to bed weary, yet I have done my work unflinchingly. I have written in bed and out of bed, written in hemorrhages, written in sickness, written torn by coughing, written when my head swam for weakness—and I have done it all for so long that it seems to me I have won my wager and recovered my glove. Yet the battle still goes on: Ill or well is a trifle so long as it goes. I was made for contest, and the Powers-That-Be have willed that my battlefield shall be the dingy, inglorious one of the bed and the medicine bottle."

Now, we might think that expression to be indicative of compulsion, endurance, courage, or skill in overcoming obstacles. It is all that, of course. But I'm suggesting it is a paragraph about the good that can come through personal trial—if we'll let it.

I'm going to share with you Ted M. Jacobsen's sensitive reflection on dealing with trauma and terrible testing. It was inspired by his sister Christine's valiant but losing battle with cancer:

"To most every life come solemn, unannounced challenges. Grave, unkind, life-critical challenges. Challenges to the depth and quality of our faith. Tearing at our heart and at the fabric of faith we've woven. We face them haltingly. Then we probe them—first testing their reality and then their resolve. We would not bid them come, or stay; for these test and plumb the very depths of our spirit. They cause at times love to contend with faith—oft times as we struggle thus to find again peace and reason, we may glimpse Gethsemane, then eternity. But as the ripples clear we sense that uninvited challenges have high, refining, eternal purpose. And 'simple' faith is not simple—but is a reflection of both heart and mind, the crown of a righteous trusting life."

I saw the stage play, then the movie, and since have lost myself in a book about a famous "elephant" man who lived near the turn of the century in England. He was a character with a soul so sensitive that his being a freak of nature for men to laugh at was more poignant than it might have been for someone less finely tuned. When he was taken from his sordid carnival environment by compassionate friends and permitted to see some of the beauties in the world, his whole being changed. He seemed nobler and more knowing than ordinary men around him did. One day he looked upon only the highest spires of the cathedral beyond the window of his confinement place, and because of the awakening of his soul he was able to build the foundation of the structure purely from his imagination. It became the pattern for his being. He saw the highest spires of his own life at last, and built a new base for his being—far loftier than the original image he had of himself as a freak of nature.

It helps if we look upon life as a preparation for the blessings of eternal life. In this way we can set our sights on different goals. Rather than looking for the happiness badge at the end of each day, we'll be more apt to look for lessons learned. Instead of complaining bitterly, or simply enduring with grace, we can grow. Instead of noisily shouting "Why me?" or "Why now?" we can declare that we are not going to blow this one chance to live by being self-pitying or sulking. We can get on with searching for the truths, the principles to help us deal with the problem appropriately so that one day this trial, too, can be counted as a blessing in disguise.

It is helpful to remember, as Paul pointed out to the Hebrews, that Christ is not unfeeling about our infirmities. He was in all points tried and tested as we are now. Yet he was without sin. He has been through it. He cares. He wants us ultimately to be like him, to make it through the trials, as he did. And he is waiting to be gracious to us.

There is a mighty promise in this scripture: "Lift up your heads and be of good comfort . . . I will also ease the burdens which are put upon your shoulders, that even you cannot feel them upon your backs, even while you are in bondage; and this will I do that ye may stand as witnesses for me hereafter, and that ye may know of a surety that I, the Lord God, do visit my people in their afflictions" (Mosiah 24:13–14).

God is able to keep his promises. He does keep them, I know. But since life is a school to learn what the Savior learned, he will not deny us our right to learn for ourselves. He blesses us not in spite of our nagging tests in life, but because of them. He loves us not because we are so great and good yet, but because he is. He is our Creator. He prescribed the principles to experience life with. He loves us and wants to help us without taking away our agency.

This is the gift.

A life's record with God in the details can be a spiritual feast for our souls. When we count our blessings on paper, our gratitude soars. It is all so evident.

FOREVER SUNSHINE

When the Lord is near, then "the dove of peace sings in my heart" and there is sunshine in my soul! What gladness to be rid of the destructive worries of the world—not spared from trouble and stress but peaceful because of living close to the Lord! What hope and happiness that there is no need to fear an enemy or the tempter! No more fretting about seeming personal inadequacy or about being in the midst of strangers or about suffering some strange sickness! It is as the Lord God said to the children of Israel, "When thou goest out to battle against thine enemies, and seest horses, and chariots, and a people more than thou, be not afraid of them: for the Lord thy God is with thee" (Deuteronomy 20:1).

Sunshine. Forever sunshine, no matter what! As long as we behave like children of Israel, followers of Christ.

That is joy.

Heavenly Father will help you make happy endings, help you enjoy exhilarating sunshine in the soul. The Lord doesn't want you held captive from him. You, through your faithfulness, are to succeed and to be happy. It is to be for you as the Psalmist said, "Thou has turned for me my mourning into dancing: thou hast put off my sackcloth, and girded me with gladness." And again, "Weeping may endure for a night, but joy cometh in the morning" (Psalm 30:11, 5).

And as for me, there is sunshine in my soul because of and in spite of—as the phrase fits—the glad happenings in life. Jesus does show his smiling face; he does raise his healing hand. He is in our midst to ameliorate our suffering, no matter what the details. Faith is the catalyst, and experience proves it so.

Now, may music begin your day and tranquility sweeten your sleep. And the next time you hear "Happy Days Are Here Again," may you sing along with gusto, knowing it is *your* song, with the encore number being "There Is Sunshine in My Soul Today."

May what Paul wrote to the Romans happen to you— may the God of hope fill you with all joy and peace in believing, that you may abound in hope, through the power of the Holy Ghost (see Romans 15:13). May you be "girded with gladness." May your cup run o'er until forever.

Sunshine. Blessed, forever sunshine!

A VIEW FROM ABOVE

Getting a view from above of what's going on below has always been fascinating for mankind. Children get excited as they dare each other to climb higher and higher in the apple tree, and little ones squeal in delight at their parents on the ground as their swing takes them up, up, and out of their parents' reach.

People peer from observation decks of skyscrapers and stop their cars at lookout spots at the Grand Canyon or Big Sur. Astronauts gaze upon earth in awe. But even before the astronauts, carrier pigeons were sent soaring with tiny cameras strapped to their breasts so that man could get a view from above the world on which he lived. The city boy from his stretching fire escape, the native boy with his towering palm tree, the sailor atop the ship's mast, get up and beyond themselves with such vantage points.

One of the favorite tourist spots near Amsterdam is the flower auction, where visitors walk blocks on narrow balconies that circle literally acres of living color in the flower stalls below. Athens from the Parthenon is a white sea as far as the eye can see. How changed the city is when one comes down to mingle in the press of people and their trappings of life!

Scanning the landscape from the window of an

in-flight mainliner is fascinating. Exquisite patterns emerge from the tapestry of a Wisconsin farmer's alfalfa field zigzagged by a narrow avenue of corn stalks. One wonders if he designed it deliberately for the passengers instead of out of some mysterious agricultural need. Pineapple fields in Hawaii laced with roads of coral sands offer a bit of beauty vastly different from Utah's dead sea, the Great Salt Lake, with its surrounding purple and gray mineral markings that frame the red patches of brine shrimp being commercially cultivated for fertilizer. Irrigation pipe tracks in Texas and Idaho have their own distinctive geometric look. The property lines of acreage in England are edged with hedges of stones varying picturesquely from the Orient's rice paddies separated by narrow canals. A California orchard of orange blossoms is a white swath compared to the Sahara's swirling sand dunes.

There is an ancient Chinese proverb that says, "If you don't scale the mountain, you can't see the plain." This is true of our lives. The view from above gives a different perspective, and if we could see ourselves as God sees us, we might work at making our lives different, even better.

I can personally recommend such activity.

I grew up in the Rockies, and our family home was on the foothill of a solitary, beehive-shaped mountain that was a moving force all of my young life. I could see it from my bedroom window and felt a certain security in its closeness. As our family sat at the kitchen table we watched winter skiers mark herringbone trails in fresh snow, and after the first thaw we'd note the progress of spring hikers. I had climbed its bald dome with my family, with church groups, and with a gang of kids (our sack lunches squashed down into the sweaters tied about our waists). Then one day, driven by desire to go to the mount like Moses and commune with God about me—to consider who I was and what I was going to do about it—I set out alone to climb that peak. I was sixteen, and this day my aloneness on the mountain was exhilarating. It was a most spectacular spring morning at sunrise when I made my way to the top. This was no small hill, so the perspective of my neighborhood below reminded me of the soap city I had carved of Salt Lake City when I was twelve.

With fascination I sat looking down at the houses I knew so well and at their people beginning to stir with the sun. Cars backed out, sprinklers splashed on, the trolley clanged up from town. I watched the achingly familiar scenes as an extension of myself. Yet, it was like being God, seeing the whole picture like that. Seeing but not being seen. I followed the paths of my life, from home to a friend's house, to the church on the corner and the school down the hill, to the neighborhood store, to a teacher who had touched me. Finally I let myself look on our own white stucco house, the scene of my most tender times, my most important learning. Almost in panic I realized how small it looked, and with a wrench of my heart I felt childhood slipping from my grasp.

Everywhere I looked there was someone who had touched my life. At sixteen I was the sum of all of them—parents, school chums, the storekeeper, church leaders. My heart flooded with a new awareness. Suddenly I realized I had some debts to pay. In 1847 Brigham Young had led a band of pioneers up to the top of that mountain and raised an ensign to the Lord, according to the plaque mounted there. Well, I raised my own standard that day and came down from the mount determined to be useful. The world seemed beautiful, and I was glad to be alive.

Remember Edna St. Vincent Millay's "Oh world, I cannot hold thee close enough"?

God created the world, and the world is an exquisite place. Getting a view from the top offers a valuable perspective of how mankind, God's ultimate creation, fits into the scheme of things.

For the song "Awakening" I wrote these words:

A GRATEFUL HEART

Who am I?
What special purpose is mine?
I follow winged sparrows
And I yearn
I yearn to soar
I hear the ocean's thunder
There is power
But what am I?
I see lilies blooming
Where the winter storms have swept the field
I feel the sun
By its radiance
I see all that God created
I, too, am God's creation
And He knows me as His own
Tenderly I know Him in my heart
Who am I?
I am a child of God.

And that lofty perspective makes all the difference.

A search of one's life and soul will reveal the
hand of God. The outpouring of his blessings
comes with our afflictions, not in spite of them.
Afflictions be praised!

"THANKS A MILLION!"

I know a very special little boy whose mother died when he was three years old. Shortly after the funeral his father had gathered the three little ones about him and was trying to help them to understand that God lived and he did love them even though their mommy had died. This father used as proof of God's love the wonders that they could see about them. He described autumn leaves, harvest foods, migrating birds, nut-gathering squirrels at their summer place, and the first snow crowning the high peaks beyond their home. One evening as he was explaining all of this, the father suddenly became aware that he had a captive audience. The boys were listening. He said to them, "Come on, let's go out into God's world and see all of this for ourselves." They all ran for their warm clothing, hurried out to the car, and then had to wait for the three-year-old, who couldn't seem to find his boots to wade through mountain snow in. But soon he came bursting out the door, threw his arms up in the air, and cried, "Oh, hello, Heavenly Father. And thanks a million."

Well, that is a great way to feel—all of our troubles and disappointments notwithstanding, thanks a million!

"COUNT YOUR MANY BLESSINGS"

Heavenly Father has amazing children on earth at this time. It has ever been so. Remember, Heavenly Father has poured out blessings upon his children under whatever circumstances in whatever age of time since Adam and Eve were cast from the gorgeous Garden and Cain killed Abel. And think of the Oklahoma bombing, Bosnia, the children of Israel in the wilderness, the pioneers in one moment burying their dead and in the next, picking up their wagons to head west. Think of people being brutally raped, ravaged, mutilated in frontier times, war zones, during the wrenching suffering and separations of the Nazi holocaust and other inquisitions, of Herod's destruction of infant boys. Think of the homeless, the beggars, the crippled, and the corrupt on the streets of the world. Think of refugees miserably trapped by political unrest and worse. Think of the repetitious exoduses of God's children over and over in the traumas of the ages.

Out of all that have come the great stories of blessings in various guises.

There are new stories in our time because God still blesses his children through the vicissitudes of life.

Clearly, counting one's many blessings is the best therapy

for overcoming *anything*. It works because it is part of our Creator's formula for our moving forward with inner peace no matter what!

Consciously and deliberately counting my own blessings has long been a healing therapy for me. I strongly recommend the method as superior for a satisfying life. We can be sick unto death, plagued with problems of all kinds, and rather than nursing a grudge, grieving over a lost love, or railing against a shortfall of some kind, remembering the blessings we do have crowds out desperation and self-pity. How sweet it is to name our blessings one by one—to literally marvel at what God has done!

The formula begins with counting the most basic blessings of life—the gift of life itself, the incredible human machine of God's design, the awesome beauty of all creation, and the grand adventure of his plan. Add to that list those fine creature comforts we enjoy in our day. For example, regardless of inevitable problems, most of us go to bed between clean sheets, have a toilet or two that flushes, a refrigerator full of a variety of FDA-protected delicacies. We have burial plots for our beloved dead. Trash removal and signals against confusion in traffic.

And we have precious relationships, including Heavenly Father and the Lord Jesus. No doubt about it, I am blessed and so are you! Thanks be to God and to each of you who act as his agents in making life more pleasant.

"GOD BLESS YOU"

I was a passenger in a car riding along a dangerously busy street in a large city where traffic in town was one big headache. The driver of the car, Kiki Knickerbocker, was an unusually chic and vibrant young mother. She also was serving as president of the stake Young Women organization. As she pulled behind several cars stopped for a red light, a street vendor waved a bottle of windshield cleaning solution and a roll of paper towels.

No one in the line of cars ahead had accepted his deal. As he approached her car—only seconds before the light changed and before she would have to move forward on her way—she rolled down her window and said, "Do what you can!"

How that man hustled to clean her windshield, even risking the traffic pattern to reach the passenger side of the windshield. She handed him a dollar, and he called, "God bless you!"

"He already has!" she called back.

A LESSON IN GRATITUDE

A friend of mine had enjoyed a rich and lengthy life with a husband who loved her and whom she adored. They had reared a fine family. Together they had buried precious loved ones and adopted a child from another race who needed a home. They had coped with financial disaster, awesome professional responsibility, some serious disappointments, and finally with sweet public success.

Then he died suddenly in his sleep. Out of the details of their life such closeness had developed that when death claimed the husband, the wife felt the sun would never shine again. She wondered that people walked the city streets smiling. She realized at last that her grief was overly long and ultimately useless, but she could not bring it to an end.

She responded to an opportunity to be a volunteer in a local pediatric hospital. Her job was to register the children being brought there for medical help. All day long she dealt with people suffering from problems, but she was oblivious to them because she still wallowed in her own grief.

One day a mother came in with a baby so deformed and pitifully stricken that my friend was startled out of her self-centered blindness. The baby's mother cheerfully reached into the heart of the grieving widow in a way that swept away bitterness and all feelings of personal uselessness. The baby's mother was a "blessing-counting" individual. She explained to the widow that she felt especially honored to be given this particularly troubled baby, this unfortunate bit of humanity to care for. "God gave this baby to me because he knew I'd love him well. Isn't that an honor for me?" This wonderful mother taught another mother the lesson of gratitude and confidence before God.

COUNT YOUR BLESSINGS AND ABIDE

We can learn from trial. We can slug it out, live it through, or wait in patience until we find the principle God has given to help us meet such a test and to gain great experience from it.

There is a powerful promise from God recorded in Doctrine and Covenants 122 upon which I based the following lines:

> *If the heavens gather blackness,*
> *If the jaws of hell gape wide,*
> *If the gaze of loved ones lowers,*

If old friends now stand aside,
If your shining dreams have vanished
And your efforts seem in vain
O keep faithful, hopeful, patient.
Rise above despair, disdain!
With God's help you can survive this—
Even flourish when you're tired.
Life is school, life is learning.
Count your blessings and abide.

A CHANGE IN ATTITUDE

Some time ago I was wheeled back into a hospital room following surgical procedures that required me to lie absolutely quiet and unmoving for eight hours. My surgeon roused me from the effects of the anesthetic and took my hand while he spoke distinctly and emphatically to be certain that I heard and understood. He told me that I must not move—no matter what—for the specified period of hours. He sternly said that my life depended upon it.

Again he asked, "Do you understand, Elaine? Your life depends upon it!"

"Easy!" I mused. Understand? Why, I welcomed such bliss. I had come into that hospital one tired lady. Eight hours of uninterrupted rest was welcome. I'd have no trouble not moving.

As soon as nurses, family, and doctor left the room, I was wide awake. Naturally, with the chance to sleep on and on, my mind wouldn't cooperate. I counted flaws in the ceiling as well as lambs in some make-believe field. Soon I ached for a more comfortable position. Later I decided that just a very slight shift in position couldn't make any difference—nobody would know . . .

Fortunately, a get-away-with-it-if-you-can attitude is a rationale that won't work when the echo of "your life depends on it" comes to mind.

So I gritted my teeth and endured, not moving. Soon my jaws ached along with the rest of my body as I lay in a flat-back position with sandbags along each side to keep me in place.

It was tough. And because what I did mattered, I prayed for help. As the hours dragged on, my own will weakened. My prayers became anxious pleas. After a time a flash of understanding came to me. Enduring—simply enduring under stress was unrewarding. I decided that the time would pass more pleasantly and profitably if I directed my thoughts. So I remembered joyful times; I counted blessings. Then I drew close to the Lord and talked some things over with him that were important to all the rest of my life.

My attitude of mere grit changed to one of willing submission geared to constructive learning. That change in attitude made all the difference in how I passed the time.

Life is like that. When we can't change a circumstance, we can either grit our teeth and hang on with clenched jaws, or we can submit cheerfully until change occurs. And with God's help we can learn some important lessons. We can feel peace.

As we look at the various kinds of trouble and stress, the trials and heartbreak that people today are tested with, some problems seem more serious and harder to take than others. But God has promised us that we will not be tested beyond what we can endure—even if we bring trouble to ourselves—because he can help us climb back out. He helps us with his principles, and he helps us with his encompassing Spirit, and he helps us through his agents.

NAME THEM ONE BY ONE

There is sunshine in my soul and gladness in my heart" are the brave words of those hardy, happy souls who see the silver lining in dark clouds and the butterfly in the fat, repulsive caterpillar on the green sprout. Such people belong to the "Men Are That They Might Have Joy" Club, and they are willing to hold out until forever to reap their reward.

In the Doctrine and Covenants the promise of joy has been defined with a timetable of *not* now and *not* in this world. We are promised a spiritual joy in Christ, and this we should seek avidly. Joseph Smith received this revelation of comfort in Kirtland, Ohio, when the Saints who had gathered in Missouri were suffering excruciating persecutions of all kinds. They were in despair. The Lord comforted Joseph, "Wherefore, fear not even unto death; for in this world your joy is not full, but in me your joy is full" (101:36). The whole plan and purpose of life is to bring about gladness in our hearts and to prepare us for an eternity of joy—ultimately, *ultimately*—when the soul and the body are interminably bonded together and capable of the fullness of joy after the manner of Christ.

Meanwhile, back on earth we reach for making the most happiness out of what we have to live with. My two grandmothers were poles apart, but I loved each of them dearly. One was generations deep in Church membership and strictness of standards. The other was a convert, an immigrant, whose small pleasures came from the beverages she'd learned to use in the old country. The first wanted me to be good. The second wanted me to be happy because she thought I *was* good. I figured this out as a young girl and marveled at how much depends on the way life is viewed. As the years passed I realized that being good brings happiness. And the grandmothers weren't so far from each other after all.

Given the parameters of mortality, given the nature of humans, given the path people tread, we must find our pleasurable moments along the way. The guide for doing this is as close as the glad tidings found in the standard works.

The scriptures speak of being "girded with gladness" and "anointed with the oil of gladness." This is highly descriptive. Indeed, why settle for a fleeting spot of happiness when you can be girded with it—swathed in it, wrapped about with it, bathed and anointed with such gladness? The imagery is akin to all the shining, smooth countenances you have ever seen; the clearest, most placid mountain lakes you've watched at sunset; the brightness and lightness and sparkle that have enhanced your memories.

But for all that, standing in front of a mirror and telling yourself, "I'm feeling glad; I'm so glad I'm feeling glad!"

doesn't necessarily make it so. Even when we ought to be happy we may instead feel jealous, angry, impatient, disappointed. Perhaps we will need to follow the pattern of Enos and Alma and even Jacob and wrestle before God for a remission of simple sins or great ones before such peace and happiness can be ours. Joy and gladness come when we have earned them, when we are prepared to receive them.

What qualities make for gladness? Peace; forgiveness, both given and received; confidence before God; virtue-garnished thoughts; principles applied; beauty in unexpected places and times, like the forgotten bulb that becomes a tulip in a compost pile—the unlooked-for blossom is a living symbol that good can spring from a dung heap.

Sometimes the innate strength and hope of a human soul surface only in times of catastrophe or unduly trying circumstances. This is so in the account of the Jaredites. They had undertaken the long and arduous journey of being blown across the sea—344 days upon the water. It must have been a most difficult trip. When at last they had landed upon the shore of the promised land and had put foot on solid ground, these valiant people "bowed themselves down upon the face of the land, and did humble themselves before the Lord, and did shed tears of joy before the Lord, because of the multitude of his tender mercies over them" (Ether 6:12).

The Jaredites are a prototype. May you be *that* glad with your own lot.

The bottom line in this life is that the closer you come to Christ and to his creations, the happier you will be. Look for the blessings and enjoy them! Then will there be sunshine in your soul no matter what lumps show up in life. There are innumerable possibilities in life that can generate happiness no matter what else is going on!

Every sunset, every winter sky, every newborn anything, every burst of apple blossoms among new green leaves, every moment of joy reflected upon or remembered is singular evidence of the wonder of all of life.

IN THE MIDST
OF AFFLICTION

---

*If we had everything that we wanted and needed
without asking of Heavenly Father, we would lose
sight of the hand of God in our lives.*

ADVERSITY
GIVES US EXPERIENCE

Adversity, well handled, can increase our understanding and compassion. When we have survived the refiner's fire, we are experienced in ways that help us to be more effective in meeting the needs of others. We learn through adversity.

"These things shall give thee experience" (D&C 122:7), the loving Lord reminds us. He knows what is good for us. He knows what help his children need. He can use us to help—and with experience we'll be more effective in service.

Adversity gives us experience. If we cope with it according to God's principles, we will find the blessings in the burdens.

It was Christmas Day 1973. Our family stood in the midst of affliction with a beloved young family member who had just learned that she was suffering from a terminal illness. There was nothing medical science could do.

Christine was the mother of three very small sons.

President Harold B. Lee was counseling with her and with us.

President Lee said to her in comfort, "Don't worry. When the Lord wants you he'll take you. And it will be all right." Looking back upon this experience, his words seem ironic because President Lee died the next day. The young mother lived for another year. But in that conversation in the Lee home, a prophet of God explained powerful principles that helped us all understand "Why me?" "Why this experience?" "Why now?" "Whatever for?" President Lee spoke of faith in God's power to perform miracles. He spoke of comfort and the peace that God could give to us if the desired miracles didn't happen. He asked our daughter-in-law if she would be willing to go through whatever was put before her, according to God's will, so that many people could learn important lessons.

In other words, would she be willing to lay down her life for others—as Christ did? That was the implication.

Her positive response was almost tentatively given. This beautiful young mother was so hopeful about being a good wife and mother. She had dreams. . . . It was difficult in the extreme to admit willingness to submit to dying, if that was the will of God.

President Lee was gentle and thoughtful as he accepted her quiet, tearful answer.

Then he said soberly, "There is so much work to do. This people are just beginning to be tested. When you are a golden nugget, prepare for the refiner's fire! Now, go home; live each day that you have according to God's will. Nothing can ultimately hurt you then."

It put a new dimension on our trouble. It fired a new resolve to keep the commandments.

Sometimes in fast and testimony meeting people will stand and share stories of miracles. For example, one person might witness that "their soldier son lived a clean life, and so he was spared, as were the sons of Helaman." And there on the next row might sit the family of a son who also lived the clean life—yet he was not spared! Did this mean God didn't love that son, his family?

In the case of Christine, she had had the best of medical help, and she had received spiritual help from President Lee. She had not given offense to the Lord in her brief life. All the family fasted, prayed, and got their lives in order. We increased our offerings and our service. There had been priesthood blessings and a crying out in faith enough to move mountains. There was her patriarchal blessing promising a long life.

Notwithstanding, Christine died.

She was honored with a beautiful funeral service. The stake center overflowed with loving, caring, and questioning people. Her young husband—our son—was chief mourner and a speaker, too. He was a great example of a believer and of one who had learned what he was supposed to learn from the trial of losing a beloved spouse.

This heartbroken husband admitted that things hadn't turned out the way he and Christine had wanted them to. But he was speaking at her funeral because it was her last request that he share their sure knowledge that God lives and loves them. This they had learned through their ordeal. It was all right. He testified of this.

It wasn't the broken heart that took center stage—difficult as this time was. It was the power and comfort of God pouring out new light and understanding upon those he loves and those whom he can use to accomplish much good among his other children.

A lot of people did learn many lessons, as President Lee suggested. After the funeral our son was repeatedly called upon to talk with people similarly tested. He could comfort with a keen compassion. He could point a way for flourishing under heartbreak. He could testify that principles applied to a problem bring forth the spirit, strength, and a sense of rightness. Such is the goodness of God.

Every burden on the back can be a gift in the hands.

"MAKE IT A GOOD DAY"

We are here on earth to be proven, here on earth to endure. Through adversity we gain valuable experience and understanding about life, principles, and the nature of God and his children. Adversity can mellow us and prepare us to draw closer to God.

Adversity proves whom God can trust.

Adversity gives us experience.

Adversity brings us closer to the Lord.

One day I was walking to work and had stopped for a traffic light. There was a strong wind whipping around the buildings. A teenage boy suddenly moved past me as I stood on the curb. He stepped into the traffic pattern, which was heavy so close to town at that hour of the day. Startled, I reached out to stop him. It was then that I realized he wasn't just a carefree youth; he was blind!

He was on his way to the blind center a block or two

further on. We walked that way together, friends now, as he said, since I had saved his life.

He explained that at the blind school he was taught to listen to the traffic pattern before he crossed the street. However, the wind that day was so severe that he couldn't hear properly, and he'd decided to take a chance. He was grateful that I was watching.

I asked him how long he'd been blind. He told me this story.

"When I was eight years old my sole purpose in life was to be the world's best and most famous baseball player," explained Glenn. "I was practicing one afternoon when a fellow player threw the bat after a hit. It landed across my eyes. This accident brought a terrible period of tribulation for my entire family.

"I was a mess," Glenn said. "I lived, but there was nothing science could do to restore my sight."

"What happened next?" I asked, intensely interested in this vigorous, handsome teenager's story.

"I withdrew from life. I sulked. I had tantrums. I wouldn't go to school. I wouldn't talk to friends. I hated my family, and I especially cried out in anger against God. I mean vocally. I would shout my hate—much to my religious mother's deep distress. This went on for many months. One day my father coaxed me into going outside with him to fly a kite. He said I'd be able to feel the tug on the kite. It would be exhilarating, even if I couldn't see it.

"We got the kite up, and I was feeling pretty good as I held the string and felt the force at work. Suddenly, the course of the breeze changed, and the kite got caught in a tree.

"I was soon out of control. I screamed and lay down on the grass and kicked. Oh, I was one ugly kid. My father called for the fire department, in desperation, I guess. They came and got the kite down, but it was broken. More tantrums from me.

"'Fix it! Fix it!' I screamed. My dad tried explaining it all to me, but I would not be comforted. It was just another of life's rotten tricks. Then Dad took my hand, and moving my fingers with his, we traced the broken crossbars of the flimsy kite.

"'See, son,' he said. 'It is broken. It can't be fixed. Like your eyes! We'll have to go and do something else.'"

The young man paused in this tracks, shook his head, remembering. Then he turned toward me and said, "That was the phrase that made the difference. 'Go and do something else.' God had given us a lot of options, and Dad would find another one for us. I'm going to the blind school now and learning a trade."

His feet had felt the pebbles laid in the concrete in front of the school as a signal for the blind people.

"I'm here," he explained confidently. "Thanks again. Make it a good day."

He didn't say, "Have a good day" as so many well-wishers do. He said, "*Make* it a good day."

With all that we have going for us, why not make it a good day? A positive approach is the beginning of winning.

One certainty is that neither here nor hereafter are we suddenly going to emerge with good qualities of character unless we have developed them. We won't reach the level of celestial living if we have not prepared ourselves.

FINDING BEAUTY AMIDST TROUBLE

How quaint a picture the flower vendor made! The cart itself spilled over with bachelor buttons, ranunculuses, African daisies, gardenias, snapdragons, roses, carnations, heather, violets, gladioli, and chrysanthemums. The flower stall was fanciful with its multicolored bric-a-brac. The genial seller of beauty and fragrance had his beret cocked over one eye and his lips pursed in a whistle. Obviously he was happy in his work.

This picture was in a travel brochure, and the enticing sales pitch for a future vacation said, "Little moments of beauty like this are apt to pop up everywhere in Europe."

Actually, little moments of beauty are apt to pop up anywhere at all in life, too. They are a valuable perk. If we'll but look for them, we'll find them, even in the midst of trouble and despair.

This personal experience may prove the point. One bleak January our family came home from a long-weekend trip and found water seeping down the basement walls and puddling the floor below. Record-breaking zero temperatures had turned the seepage into tiny sheets of ice wherever the water had traveled.

Naturally my husband and I were horrified. The children, however, quickly squealed in delight at frozen patterns marking the concrete and unfamiliar icicles clinging to the rough sides of the unfinished basement walls.

"It's a frost garden," laughed four-year-old Susan. "Jack Frost has been here. He's been inside our very house. Look!"

Our little artist went scurrying to examine and point out to the rest of us the "frost garden" flowers, ferns, and spikes.

Susan saw the beauty. I saw that these frozen designs were splitting the concrete, sogging the carpet, matting the stuffed animals of the play area, and inevitably creating more work for Mother and Dad.

But to see beauty in a time of trauma stimulates hope for better times.

It's easy to see beauty in the stretch of pink blooms of a peach orchard in early spring. But to see chic monochromatic beauty instead of boring sameness as one looks across a winter field, snow drifted against the beige stakes of a barbed wire fence and beyond, the nakedness of poplars marking the border from mountain to highway, it takes quite another sort of eye—and heart. How much better it is for one's disposition to be such a beholder of beauty.

Applied to the times of affliction in our lives, we can soften our suffering if we search for the good and, yes, the beautiful in a time of sickness and affliction.

ADVERSITY PROVES WHOM GOD CAN TRUST

Adversity proves whom God can trust. Who of us, as Job did, will stand firm, be obedient, and love God no matter what comes into our lives? We are proven through adversity.

A few years ago I was talking with some people of Rexburg, Idaho, about the devastating flood following the bursting of the Teton Dam.

The story of one woman is especially interesting in terms of this chapter's focus. I asked this woman if her family had been seriously affected by the flood. She drove me to a hill overlooking the city to which citizens had rushed when the flood warning was given. From there they could watch the wide path of raging water and follow the destruction of their own homes in its wake.

"Yes," she exclaimed, "we were seriously affected. But first let me give you some background."

Then she told me that the family had struggled for years to get adequate housing for their growing family. At last there came a day when a fine house was finished with appropriate bedrooms and storage. They had worked out a remarkable facility for their year's supply of food and commodities.

One morning shortly before dawn broke, they smelled smoke. Their new home on rural acreage was consumed by flames. The fire took everything but their lives and the night clothing they were wearing. Everything—including the food storage gathered at the counsel of a prophet.

"But, Sister Cannon, it was wonderful to see the Lord's blessings unfold," she continued. "Before the day was over we had clothes to wear and places to sleep with neighbors. Within a year we were able to build another house and fill it with our children and our newly acquired year's supply of staples."

"That is wonderful," I agreed.

"Yes, but shortly after we moved in, the Teton Dam broke. We were right in the path of that raging, mile-wide broom that swept this valley clean. From this hill where we stand, we watched our house go. We had binoculars, but because we were crying they weren't much good."

A neighbor who didn't understand gospel principles had scoffed at this family's futile preparations for some future time. When trouble came, their food storage had burned or washed away. Now that neighbor said to the family, "What good is it to collect all that food storage, all those emergency supplies? If you go through that ridiculous process again, that is your business, but don't tell me about it. It hasn't done you any good. Why go to that trouble if you can't eat it when you need it?"

My friend was thoughtful before such an accusation. Then she firmly replied, "Nobody told me I had to eat it."

And she is right; she had been told only to store it, and she had been obedient. In spite of adversity her spirit was sweet.

I thought of Joseph Smith's response to trouble during a certain period of his life. It was 1842, just two years before he was murdered by his enemies. He was in hiding and wrote:

> And as for the perils which I am called to pass through, they seem but a small thing to me, as the envy and wrath of man have been my common lot all the days of my life; . . . God knoweth all these things. . . . Deep water is what I am wont to swim in. It all has become a second nature to me; and I feel, like Paul, to glory in tribulation; for to this day has the God of my fathers delivered me out of them all, and will deliver me from henceforth; for behold, and lo, I shall triumph over all my enemies, for the Lord God hath spoken it. [D&C 127:2]

Like Joseph we can triumph over our enemies, surmount our problems. We can do it with God's help.

Spiritual maturity is understanding that we cannot
blame anybody else for our problems.

RETURNING GOOD FOR EVIL

Judy Thompson's family was not stricken by war or public bombings but their suffering nonetheless had been
acute. When their problems began they were living in a
small Ohio town where everyone went to the one and only
Protestant church to play bingo on Saturday nights for
pocket change; then back they'd go again on Sunday to worship. Usually the same people showed up for both occa-
sions, and Judy's family was part of that crowd. Then Judy's
husband, Brett, met a fine man who was a bank loan officer
in a larger city nearby. Brett was trying to get a loan to build
an addition to their house. The twin girls were nearly ten
years old now and needed a room apart from their older
brother. Mr. Rawson asked Brett many questions about his
life, his values, his family. Approved, Brett received the loan.
In addition, the two men found that they had much in common, and before long the Thompson family was driving
over to the Rawson home each week to meet with the LDS
missionaries for gospel instruction. They even attended

church services in that city a time or two before they were baptized. As often as they could, the Thompsons happily drove the distance to the city for church with the Mormons.

Soon trouble began among their neighbors in the small town where they lived. Resentment built up over their conversion. The children were not welcome in the home of their friends, and they were beaten up at school. Robert even lost his job as delivery boy for the pharmacist. Brett and Judy were not invited to social events; they couldn't even get appointments at the barber and beauty shop! The gas station wouldn't service the car. The owner of the grocery store deliberately turned his back and walked away when any of the family came in for supplies. It was a miserable time. The only thing that had changed was their understanding of God and the plan of life, and yet no one—not a soul—would speak to any family member.

"We cried out to the Lord to show us the way," Judy said. "We clung to each other and made excuses for our neighbors. We put our house up for sale, and garbage was thrown on the porch. Rocks broke our windows. Imagine that kind of prejudice in this day and age. We wondered what we had gotten ourselves into.

"The children wanted to give up this new church because their friends had told them that was the problem.

It was truly awful," added Judy. "A spirit of darkness and despair was surrounding us all. At first we were too embarrassed to mention our problem to our new Mormon friends at the church in the city where Brett now worked."

Judy continued, "One day the bishop drove all the way out to our home to keep an appointment. He told us about the people in Alma's day who had suffered so greatly at the hands of their enemies. When they couldn't stand it any longer, he said, they began to cry out mightily to God, just as we had been doing. The bishop had us turn to our scriptures and read the following passage from Mosiah 24:13–15: 'And it came to pass that the voice of the Lord came to them in their afflictions, saying: Lift up your heads and be of good comfort, for . . . I will . . . ease the burdens which are put upon your shoulders, that even you cannot feel them upon your backs, even while you are in bondage; . . . the burdens which were laid upon [them] were made light; yea, the Lord did strengthen them that they could bear up their burdens with ease, and they did submit cheerfully and with patience to all the will of the Lord.'"

Judy's story ended with a beautiful testimony. The bishop called their attention to the next verses in that chapter, which reminded this fine family that God does visit his people in their afflictions. They are not forgotten.

This he does because of covenants made and also so that they will be witnesses to others of God's goodness!

Judy's family knelt in prayer, and the bishop asked Heavenly Father to protect each family member and to bless the home. He asked that they might be guided with ideas about appropriate ways to rebuild friendships so that hearts in the town could be softened and the work of the Lord could go forward.

Judy said, "We continued to return good for evil and to do all kinds of Christian service, like getting up early to secretly shovel a neighbor's pathways or to chop wood for a widow's wood-burning stove or to make tiny cakes for a wedding we were not invited to. We now know four other people who have seen the missionaries and have been baptized. We *know* that the Lord lives and answers prayers. We are witnesses to that. We are happier than ever before now."

We do not know what we have to go through to get where we are meant to be! Heavenly Father yearns for our success in life and our safe return to his presence.

THE GREAT ONES
STRETCH ABOVE IT

Studying people who are struggling can be motivating. For example, there was a gentle, wholesome woman whose husband became involved in a financial scam. They were publicly disgraced and impoverished. How did she react? She kept her pleasant demeanor by pushing her inner strength into gear. She let no one know how deeply she was hurting. She took action, too, carrying two morning newspaper routes. She shared portions of her journal with me for that period. It included an accounting of the family finances, which showed a steadily growing bank account from the money made delivering papers before others were awake. Her conquering spirit heightened her self-esteem; newfound value within her brought a kind of happiness and a sense of well-being.

Small souls shrink with trouble, but great ones stretch above it.

FOR OUR ETERNAL GOOD

Recently I sat in sacrament service and pondered the sacrifice of Jesus. I wondered, too, about the bitter cup my husband and I had been pressed into taking lately. It was little compared to the cup of our Lord, but we had struggled and suffered, fasted, prayed, waited. No answer. There was the despair, the tears, the sleepless nights with pacing and praying, the scripture study, the striving for patience. There were times of counseling together as well as listening to others who had endured similar heart-ripping trauma. Finally, when the resolution of a trial—a test—came, we were grateful that we had survived the traumatic time with our faith intact. In fact, we were filled with a new closeness to God. On this particular day I took the sacrament in humility and gratitude for his suffering for us. How good God is. We had felt his sustaining presence even while he *allowed* us to go through an ordeal in order for us to grow. I was thankful as well that we hadn't made a bigger problem for ourselves by not being trustworthy. Giving up, complaining in self-pity, questioning—in any way turning away from God is not appropriate for one who has made sacred covenants!

I took the sacrament that day with a new commitment

to the Lord's work, to the plan and the principles. In spite of—perhaps even because of—sadness and agony in trial, I could praise God.

Struggle proves the presence, the reality of Christ, his mission, and his sacrifice for us. Surely, with such a gift to us we should be trustworthy before God.

God will help us in a variety of ways. He has told us that by doing the things we are supposed to do when we are supposed to do them, the "gates of hell shall not prevail against you; yea, and the Lord God will disperse the powers of darkness from before you, and cause the heavens to shake for your good" (D&C 21:6).

The gospel is more than a system of ethics. It is doing—experimenting upon the word, living according to God's way and his will. That means all the time, in good times and bad times alike. It means working with increasing effectiveness to keep from bringing trouble upon ourselves by not living the gospel, by turning blessings into burdens.

But however trials come, all of them can give us experience and be for our eternal good.

COME AND GET IT!

Another trial that might cause us to weep is a forced move. Breaking up a family home usually breaks somebody's heart. So much that has meant security, tradition, identity, and happiness is sifted, sorted, boxed up, portioned off, or cast away. Tears are shed as memories surface. Traumatic decisions must be made.

What can be the blessing behind this kind of adversity? Where can comfort come in such a threatening change? What attitude or course of behavior can dry the weeping eye?

Financial disaster wiped out the resources of our family. We were forced to move from our three-story home to an apartment. Conditions would be crowded at best, so we couldn't take most of our belongings.

Years of family growing, celebrating, serving, studying, and acquiring cluttered each room and storage place. We now had to make decisions about every item.

After a family counsel—a prayer and a rehearsal of God's ultimate purpose for his children—we decided that instead of having a commercial yard sale, we would share the things we couldn't use—the treasures as well as the "precious trash." In our time of unhappiness, we could bring delight to others.

We held a come-and-get-it-affair. We did it in style, too. The dining room table was spread with the best cloth, baked pastries, and lemonade. Blossoms from the garden banked the entrance hall. It was a festive time.

Neighbors, close friends, and extended family members of all ages were invited to wander through the various bedrooms to see displays of the items to be given away. Guests could choose to take whatever they wanted! Books and records were available in the library. Games and hobby equipment were found in the family room. And so it went, all through the house.

Of course, people were startled—almost disbelieving—at first. But soon it was fun—and a very practical solution to our problem. People not only left that family home laden with gifts, but they also had an idea of what one might do about certain kinds of adversity in order to turn tears into joy. It was a time of remembering God's goodness, too, and it was a time of heartwarming exchange. This had been a happy home where good lessons were learned right up to the last day. "Out of the abundance of the heart," indeed!

Severe trouble tends to underscore the kind of relating

people engage in. Our family was active in the Church. We supported each other in Church-related duties as well as in the chores about the house or in the community that were required of us. We loved each other, and when trouble came we were bound even more closely together. Of course, everyone felt brokenhearted about leaving the family home. Admittedly, tears came easily until we hit upon our plan to bring joy to others. That plan turned the whole experience around. The remarkable thing is that down the road several years, what had seemed a terrible burden and disappointment (breaking up and leaving behind our family home), proved to be a powerful preparation for other more challenging experiences family members later faced.

Rather than just shedding tears, strive for gratitude— for a chance to grow closer to God, to prove worthy of his trust, to learn lessons that can help us help others. This should be our attitude and goal. Yes, this is more easily said than done, especially at first, but with proper practice we can become good at flourishing under adversity.

PROMISES AND
PINK CARNATIONS

When our neighbor Dorothy came to Church bravely wearing a corsage she'd made from her husband's funeral roses and gladioli, people were surprised. It was so soon.

Dorothy and Smitty had been a happily married young couple. For the teenagers in the neighborhood they were the ideal of a romantic marriage. They had several little children and a new home with a garden in back and chairs on the front porch to welcome the people who dropped by to visit the popular family.

Then Smitty's health began to fail, until finally heart surgery was performed—unsuccessfully. Now, only a day or two after the funeral, Dorothy stood in testimony meeting to declare her faith in God. She began by telling this little riddle:

Q. If all the people who were sick and afflicted were given a pink Cadillac, what kind of country would this be?

A. A pink carnation.

She explained that a little girl sitting there behind her in church had noticed that Dorothy was sad and tearful through the meeting. Her little girl's heart wanted to help.

She thought of her favorite riddle and hoped it would brighten Dorothy's mood. She leaned forward across the church pew and whispered it to Dorothy.

It worked. That light approach gave Dorothy the moment she needed to shake the sadness, to stand with a smile, and speak of the promises she already had seen fulfilled from God. Even though Smitty no longer lived on earth, even though her prayers hadn't been answered the way she had hoped they would, she testified that she had been comforted, filled with peace from God that was real and powerful.

Dorothy told the congregation about the dear child who had shared the pink carnation story. She said, "I am grateful to God, too, for thoughtful people like my little friend, who was quick to see my need and try to be helpful in some way. It has helped me remember that we all can be instruments in the hands of God to bring forth his promises of solace and hope."

I never see a bouquet of pink carnations without being reminded of that sweet moment in a testimony meeting. For example, I went to the mortuary to support the parents of a three-month-old baby girl lying in a tiny casket with a bouquet of pink and white carnations resting on the top. This baby was the long-awaited joy of their hearts.

There would be no more children in that family, and the mother's heart was broken. She struggled with her questions and her anger that her prayers had been ignored. She felt rejected by heaven. And it hurt.

I told the distraught mother about Dorothy and her little six-year-old friend a row back in church with the riddle of the pink carnations. She turned and fingered the lovely pink bouquet blanket over the beloved baby. She smiled at the simple humor and said, "Aren't children wonderful? They can restore our perspective in a hurry. Just knowing that people care about us in a time of sadness has a way of reminding us that surely God cares, as well."

And of course, he does.

So take heart if you are feeling forgotten. Take heart no matter how bad things seem for the moment.

There is a scripture that can make your day brighter because it carries a message of hope and promise. In the first and second verses of section 98 of the Doctrine and Covenants the Lord reminds us, "Verily I say unto you [verily means *in truth*, you know] my friends [he calls us his friends!], fear not, let you hearts be comforted; yea, rejoice evermore, and in everything give thanks; waiting patiently on the Lord, for your prayers have entered into the ears of the Lord of Sabaoth, and are recorded with this seal and testament—the Lord hath sworn and decreed [promised!] that they shall be granted."

You can't have a better promise than that.

This is the challenge of life: To see how much we can endure of defeat and heartbreak and still come forth intact.

HOPE WIPES OUT WORRY

The truth is that when you look for a scripture to solve a certain problem, you find so many wonderful thoughts on a variety of other subjects that hope wipes out worry. On the other hand, there is one scripture that fills my heart with sadness when people do not live by scriptural standard. It is the setting where the Nephites had become a sinful and warring people and wanted Mormon to lead them, one more time, against their enemies, the Lamanites. In response, Mormon took *all* the precious records and buried them against destruction. Finally he agreed to lead their forces forth. "But behold," he records, "I was without hope, for I knew the judgments of the Lord

225

which should come upon them; for they repented not of their iniquities, *but did struggle for their lives without calling upon that Being who created them"* (Mormon 5:2; emphasis added).

Let it not be said of us that we were too foolish to get help from our Creator, who, according to his own word, is waiting to be gracious to us. Seeking and learning of God and his purposes "by study and also by faith" (D&C 109:7) is the way to successfully deal with life's most traumatic challenges.

During my husband's long, final illness we still studied the scriptures together. We pleasured in the word of God by noting language, symbolism, parallelism, and finding a chiasmus or coincidence. When Jim could no longer take a turn reading, he chose the scripture, and I would remind him of when he had used the scripture in a talk, a funeral address, or an essay. He would smile and nod at the memory. Even the memory of a scripture experience was a lovely thing in a life however narrowed by circumstance. When I read the scriptures out loud, I read with as much beauty of expression as my language-loving mother would approve. I also read to her before she died. I was amazed that though she was too weak to open her eyes, she followed the text intently. If I paused a moment to get my breath or perhaps to test if she were sleeping, Mother would pick up where I left off, complete the Article of Faith, recite the rest of a phrase in 3 Nephi 17, or complete the paragraph in Joseph Smith History. She had been an apt scholar of the scriptures in word and in life.

Sometimes our list of anguish was longer than usual. Often it included the special needs of friends and loved ones. We learned another truth: with a pile-up of problems God has our full attention, so we learn more. We search the scriptures. We search our own souls for signs of unworthiness or the need to repent—have we been slow to hearken unto the voice of the Lord our God? This stunning scripture inevitably comes to mind when our need is great *now:* "In the day of their peace they esteemed lightly my counsel; but, in the day of their trouble, of necessity they feel after me" (D&C 101:8).

The longer I live the clearer the vision becomes of how God's plan for us is peppered with a variety of trials to push us to our limit, either by the nature of the problem, the cost of it, or the unrelenting assault of all kinds of struggles. When the ultimate grief strikes—and when it strikes again and then again—it is a wake-up call to look for the lesson and learn!

I went through a close series of deaths, which took

both of my brothers, my daughter, my son, and my husband in a tight period of time. Meanwhile, for a season I fought for my own life. Along the way, through the illness, the dying, and the deaths, I discovered Mosiah 24:12–16. It was a neon-light moment. That is a scripture to share, to reapply to yet another type of trial. Alma and his people were in deep anguish, and so great were their afflictions because of their enemy that they did not only "raise their voices to the Lord their God, but did pour out their hearts to him; and he did know the thoughts of their hearts" (v. 12). What solace that sentence brings! The story unfolds, "And it came to pass that the voice of the Lord came to them in their afflictions, saying: Lift up your heads and be of good comfort . . . and I will also ease the burdens which are put upon your shoulders, that even you cannot feel them upon your backs" (vv. 13–14).

This promise worked for me. I did not feel the burden of being an ill woman who was at once slave laborer, caregiver, and cheerleader to loved ones in need. If they did it in the Book of Mormon, I could do as much in my day of crying out. Besides, I could go to bed between clean sheets laundered in my spiffy spinner.

But there was more that I learned, thanks be to Heavenly Father.

The Lord strengthened Alma's people, and he counseled them to stand as witnesses for him that it would be known abroad that he does visit his people in their afflictions (see v. 14). Also, we his people are to submit "cheerfully and with patience to all the will of the Lord" (v. 15).

The positive marching orders to "lift up your heads, be of good comfort" and the assurance that the pain would be over because the dear Lord would get involved has helped me again and again. I cannot begin to express the smallest part of what I feel in gratitude to the Lord for such scriptures, which give us particular access to him.

THROUGH
HUMBLE PRAYER

---

*Unless inside, where no one sees, our soul is
kneeling, too, a prayer is not so likely to go through.*

JESUS LISTENING CAN HEAR

A season ago our lovely daughter was fighting for her life. Her disease was one of the strange new ones that would not be diagnosed until the autopsy was performed. She did not want to die. She had a young family. She had a satisfying and important Church calling and a beautiful new home. She had faith, and she engaged in a great deal of secret prayer. She sought anointing and administration from the priesthood.

During an illness it often helps to be engaged in a project to keep the mind occupied and the hours in bed profitable, and this young mother used her enviable creative skills to work her belief into a pillow. "Do Not Doubt!" she boldly worked in beautiful needlepoint letters across the canvas. In her hospital room, that pillow had a place of honor for all to see—beloved nurses, honored doctors, technicians, visitors, and her family. She'd tried to get her life in order to be worthy of the miracle. And she did not doubt. She was claiming her blessings—as she wanted them. Now she thought that all she had to do was be patient until the miracle happened.

As she steadily worsened, I became very concerned. I wondered if she would die being angry at God, and I couldn't stand that. My own prayers changed then. I prayed for God's will in the matter of her sickness and her life-span agenda, of course. But now I also prayed fervently for a light to fill her, that whatever the outcome, it would be recognized as a blessing and the will of God. *That* prayer of mine was answered. In a very sacred moment our daughter was caught up in the Spirit and allowed to discuss the timing of her death and its purpose. I was with her and saw her transfigured, if you will. She was filled with light, and never in her life was she more lovely and radiant. She lived three or four more months in peaceful acceptance and in an attitude of preparation for leaving her family and moving on.

There is a definition in the LDS Bible Dictionary that is important to note as we try to understand the avenue to God that is ours: "Prayer is the act by which the will of the Father and the will of the child are brought into correspondence with each other. The object of prayer is not to change the will of God, but to secure for ourselves and for others blessings that God is already willing to grant, but that are made conditional on our asking for them. Blessings require some work or effort on our part before we can obtain them.

Prayer is a form of work, and is an appointed means for obtaining the highest of all blessings" (pp. 752–53).

We know God lives and hears our prayers. Perhaps we don't always realize this wonder in our lives because often we are looking for some other blessing than that which we have at hand. The privilege of sacred prayer is to draw close to God. He already knows the desires of our hearts, but a change must occur within us; having been passive we become active through prayer. Prayer is, indeed, a boon for us. For a choice lift, sing again the old-fashioned, heartwarming lines:

> *There is an hour of peace and rest,*
> *Unmarred by earthly care;*
> *'Tis when before the Lord I go,*
> *And kneel in secret prayer.*
> *May my heart be turned to pray,*
> *Pray in secret day by day,*
> *That this boon to mortals giv'n*
> *May unite my soul with heav'n.*
>   *[Hans Henry Petersen,*
>   *"Secret Prayer," Hymns, no. 144]*

Being united with heaven is what gladness is really all about. When this condition exists, regardless of the terrifying or stressful details of life, everything will ultimately be happy and fine. We go before the Lord faithfully and cheerfully, and Jesus listening can hear!

A LESSON IN FAITH

Scott parked the car in the driveway closer to the street than the house. There were toys and equipment strewn up ahead. It had been a busy day for the "troops," as he referred to his family of three sons. There was a baby girl in their family, too, but she was still a harmless babe in arms. His annoyance was softened toward the children when he noticed the "replica helmet" Jason had begged for to wear on his Big Wheel so he'd feel as grown up as the bigger boys. Scott couldn't stay burned by the boys' antics for long when the Lord had given him such fine ones.

Scott honked the car horn a couple of times, but no one rushed to move the toys so he could pull into the garage. That was a rule to which little attention was given, obviously. Rather than disturb the neighbors with his honking, he turned off the motor and gathered his day-planner to go inside the house. He would roust them out to move their play gear and put the car away later.

Scott loved being a father. Primarily that was because

his own father had loved being a father, as he constantly declared in word and deed. Pop had advised Scott when the first baby came that the years went far too fast, so he had better make the most of fatherhood while influence over his children was still possible. *Influence?* thought Scott. *I haven't even been able to get them to put their stuff away at the end of play.*

Inside there was trauma, and Will raced to meet him when he shut the front door. The boy was crying and tugged on his pant leg to direct him toward the master bedroom. There was a scene to break any father's heart. Toddler Jason was flat on the bed, white and still. Mom sat beside him, gently rubbing her hand across his chest. Baby Lily, who obviously had been hurriedly plopped on the big bed, kicked and screamed. Everybody else shouted in anxiety over Jason. "Dad! Is Jason dead?" "Dad, save Jason!" "Jason can't breathe, Dad!" "Save him, save him." "We've called 911," his wife interjected, "but what if he dies first? He fell backwards from the Big Wheel, and he isn't breathing." Then there was a chorus of, "Pray over him, Dad."

Scott ran to the top of the medicine cabinet and took the consecrated oil from its special box. Without really knowing any details of the problem, he asked the boys to fold their arms for prayer. He directed his weeping wife to kneel down beside the bed. He put his hands on the ailing boy's head, but for a few moments he couldn't speak. His thoughts raced. Jason threatened? Lose Jason? Could he demand of God that Jason rise and walk? Scott silently, fervently cried out to heaven for faith instead of fear as he performed the ritual of a father's blessing for Heavenly Father's spirit child. In moments his spirit calmed, and he felt the warm confirmation surge through his body as he blessed Jason to awaken and be healed, by the power of the holy priesthood of God vested in him. He had battled with even saying the words "Thy will be done" before he closed the blessing, but then he knew his prayer had been heard. There was a murmured "amen!" from Jason as Scott lifted his hands from his injured son's head. He felt a new lump well up in his own chest to see his little sons still in the reverent mood of prayer with their arms folded, their eyes scrunched shut. Of course Heavenly Father couldn't resist such pleadings from such devoted boys.

Suddenly Scott knelt down next to his wife beside the bed and guided the boys to do the same. Again he addressed Heavenly Father in prayer. This time he spoke as a father of a family grateful beyond expression to *be* a family, grateful for abundant blessings, including trust in a loving Heavenly Father. Especially, they took time for a formal thanks to God for rousing Jason. *If I feel as I do about Jason,* thought Scott, *how much more must a good and perfect being like God love him!* All would be well, and the faith of the kneeling brothers would not be destroyed. They'd one day learn about putting toys away, but through a lesson in faith like this immediate answer to prayer, they would be helped along the road toward being loving fathers themselves.

The mental picture of old father Jacob and his sons gathered in Egypt, reunited with beloved Joseph is a commanding one. They had been separated as a family since Joseph as a youth had been sold into Egypt as a slave by jealous brothers. Here is a scriptural account that every father would benefit from by following and taking it up as a blessing in life to enhance his understanding of fatherhood. For Jacob is indeed an example of faith! He pronounced a father's blessing upon the head of each of his sons, the scripture points out, telling them individually "that which shall befall [them] in the last days" (Genesis 49:1).

"I NEED HELP"

One cries out to God for help, and sometimes he sends it through an earth angel. In certain kinds of situations it takes at least two people with God to bring relief. One prays, God listens, and the helper must be in tune with the silent throbbing of instruction from heaven to meet a need. God often works his wonders through the life and goodness of a person sensitive to inspiration. He draws near to us after we have decided to draw near to him.

Tracy was a young mother, inexperienced but willing. She was currently serving as stake Young Women president. As the time drew near for annual camp, Tracy had been pleased with the plans until the camp director's life took a sudden turn, and at almost the last minute she was forced to drop out of the picture that year. Full responsibility for the complicated event fell upon Tracy. Everything was in order, however—the camp site was reserved, the assignments had been made, the girls had earned their fees and were practically packing their duffel bags. Then suddenly, two weeks before camp time, the facility closed down. Tracy tried every angle she could think of to relocate the camp. She really feared disappointing the girls;

and more important, camp was the time when lives changed with thought-provoking talk around the campfire, and leaders and girls bonded with the good spirit present out in nature.

With her resources exhausted, Tracy sat in church contemplating the way she could soften the blow of announcing the cancellation that day. Suddenly, the words of the congregational song touched her. Tracy emphasized, "I was mumbling along with 'Ere you left your room this morning, did you think to pray?' when I *heard* the words sharply and *saw* the words flash across the monitor of my mind! It was a clear message to me that I'd tried everything that I could do, but I hadn't tried getting help from Heavenly Father. I hadn't turned over the problem involving his girls to *him!*"

Tracy slipped out of the meeting and found a quiet place to kneel in prayer. Embarrassed because she hadn't specifically prayed over this situation before, Tracy humbly admitted an urgent need of heaven's help, not for herself but for a wonderful group of daughters of God. Almost immediately the idea came to her to telephone a certain woman. "I don't know why I am calling you," explained Tracy to the woman who answered the telephone later. "But I need help!" When the story of the canceled camp unfolded, the woman stopped Tracy and said, "Really? I have been praying about what I could do with a prepaid, no-refund-for-cancellation campsite where our extended family reunion was to be held next week. Circumstances have changed, and I'm left holding the bag!" The two women proclaimed each other an answer to prayer. They laughed and wept together, marveling at God's help in bringing them together.

At camp the chorister led the girls in the verses of "Come, Come, Ye Saints." When they sang the words "We'll find the place which God for us prepared," the stake Young Women president wept openly. In her opening greeting she testified that Heavenly Father still cared about the details in life, and she described how God had helped them find a proper place for camp. Tracy added later, "Why didn't I think of the avenue of prayer sooner and save myself so much grief and worry?"

THE PEAR TREE

As you exercise faith in Christ through your need, self-discipline, and righteousness, you will not only become an even better person, but your faith will increase.

The following is a true account of an incident that I witnessed, and I have written it as accurately as I could, to catch the fact and spirit of what happened. There are many fine lessons to consider in this story.

She stood in fast and testimony meeting on a fall day, a neighbor we'd known long and admired. Her hands, curled over the pew against which she leaned, showed the comfortable evidence of hard work in life. Her hair now was nearly all white, only peppered with dark on the springy, wiry strands casually knotted on the crown of her head. She spoke in a gentle, well-modulated voice, and her bright eyes reflected her intelligent interest in things. Anna spoke matter-of-factly when she said, "I would like the children of this ward to hear the story of the miracle of the pear tree. It is a true story that happened to me this year. It was my pear tree.

"Most of you know where I live. It has been our family home for forty years. There we struggled with our trials and welcomed our joys. And the pear tree was one of my joys. When the children were young we were having our trials. It was hard getting enough food for growing young bodies. We had planted a Bartlett pear tree. Our front yard had the best sun exposure, and so that tree grew right from the grassy stretch of parking between the street and sidewalk. We watched it flourish and produce more pears each years. It gave us hope and gladness all those years. It also gave us pears.

"But for a long time that pear tree has been nothing more than a nuisance. Those of you who walk by our house might have wondered why I didn't cut it down. The budding fruit, hard like little rocks, would drop all over the ground and sidewalk. People would trip over them or turn an ankle. The fallen pears would clutter the gutter, creating a backlog of debris that caused floods in rainstorms.

"One day this past spring my spirits were so low that I got myself out of the house. I walked toward the pear tree and wept a bit as I recalled the fruitful years when bottled pears had pleasured our lives and given us sustenance. Suddenly, my need for sustenance right then was so great that I bowed my head and prayed. Then I looked up into heaven and quietly sang out, 'O God, bless the pear tree! Bless the pear tree that it may yield good fruit.' And now I have forty quarts of bottled pears on the shelves in my basement. And I want the children of this ward to hear about the miracle of the pear tree so that they would know that God lives and answers prayers."

That same evening we were invited to a social gathering

with people who had been in the congregation at fast and testimony meeting. Someone raised a question about the "miracle of the pear tree." The discussion was lively, and the mood was decidedly skeptical. "She probably pruned and watered the old pear tree, gave it a shot or two of fertilizer," observed a well-known attorney. Similar comments from other distinguished citizens were tossed on the Discredit Heap.

I was annoyed at what was going on. Hadn't any of these people ever been close enough to the Spirit to recognize the faith of this woman? I took courage and spoke up. "All right. Show of hands—how many of us pruned and watered and fertilized our pear trees this year?" Several hands were raised. "And how many of you were blessed with a bumper crop of pears—worth forty quarts?"

All hands dropped to laps as people looked about at each other in astonishment. Nobody in that neighborhood had any pears. Though we had pruned and watered, there was no miracle in our own orchards because a killer frost had nipped our fruit trees in the bud last spring.

When true faith is present, God blesses with miracles, with ministering angels, with spiritual gifts, with every conceivable good thing. Our prayers are heard and noted, and signs follow the believers!

*Through prayer, our agency is used
to admit and confess our deep desire to have
God's help in our lives.*

PRIESTHOOD BLESSINGS

It is blessings all around when one is ordained with the power and keys to bring good from God to others, or to be on the receiving end. To be blessed with protection or enhancement in a life situation is to be lifted in soul and body, and to become happily indebted to God.

Pause now for a mind-picture of an authorized agent of God laying hands upon the head of someone you love and, by virtue of the priesthood of God in him vested, and in the name of Jesus Christ, pronouncing a blessing for the well-being of that loved one. It is the picture of service, love, faith, hope, and the link of God, man, and a needful one. It is the ultimate beautiful mind-picture reaffirming that God does not leave his children on earth unattended. The following examples may bring personal remembrance of such moments.

A newborn is cradled in his father's arms and encircled about by grandfathers, other priesthood members in the family, the bishopric, home teachers, and perhaps even the doctor who delivered him into the world. That baby is given a name by which he will be known on the records of the Church and the land. The newborn is enriched by a proud father who rightfully pronounces a blessing that echoes the throbbing desires in his heart for the lifetime of this little one. The baby isn't the only one blessed either, though the hands are laid upon its head. Those in the circle of prayer, the mother, those listening beside her—all are blessed in this participation-in-yearning for a new member of the human race.

Cindy was given up for adoption by her unwed birth mother. The attorney who handled the adoption, bringing the baby into a home of faith and obedience, was invited to be part of the momentous occasion of the naming and blessing of Cindy by her new father. Such was their gratitude to the man who prayerfully sought proper placement for this spirit child of God. That Cindy belonged in their home was confirmed by a thundering spiritual evidence in the soul during the ordinance.

Eight-year-old A. J. was radiant as he sat encircled by priesthood brethren with their hands placed upon his head to confirm him and bestow upon him the gift of the Holy Ghost. He was excited and thrilled and tried to control his joyous smile. Following the prayer, the men each extended a handshake of welcome as A. J. moved about the circle. When he reached his father, A. J. suddenly dropped the formalities and hugged him about the waist. In a clear rush of emotion, the young father tightened his arms about the boy.

Repeated in good homes is the father's blessing given to a bride-to-be daughter on her wedding eve—this grown man with tears running down his cheeks as he blesses his forever "little pink-cheeked cherub" (as he always called her) before turning her over to the arms of her young husband for care and keeping. (He silently wonders—good as the young man might be, is he good enough?)

Daddy was stretched out on a hospital bed, frighteningly unfamiliar, connected with tubes, cords, machines, and bottles of mysterious fluids. Mother and her children knelt by the bedside, the memory fresh of years of family prayer side by side. Rick called down the powers of heaven to look in mercy upon this little family: "According to thy will, O Father, please heal, comfort, enlighten, and sustain this precious group gathered here in faith, that whatever is ahead we may trust in thee and feel thy blessed closeness, knowing thy goodness and mercy all the days of life." Each rose to kiss Daddy—tears washing the benevolent ritual of farewell.

"It is all right," the balding, ailing cancer victim whispered reassuringly. And it was.

A PRAYER FOR OUR HOME

Because we don't always know what is in store for us, cultivating proper prayer, drawing close to God even when circumstances of life aren't particularly demanding, can prepare us for inevitable problems along life's path. We are already in touch with God.

Our family knelt around the master bed during a period when all of the children were home. There were eight of us then whose lives were inextricably intertwined by birth, choice, and temple sealing. We had just moved from our crowded little house to a larger but shabbier place. Our work was cut out for us, and our budget was tight. We had discussed these realities of our lives one more time just before we knelt to pray.

We wanted this move and the risks involved to be right for us, of course.

We wanted all things pertaining to this change in our lives to be according to God's will for our family.

We wanted his watch over our investment.

We wanted the Holy Spirit to dwell there and per-
meate our lives.

We wanted protection and peace.

But we also wanted our house to be handsome one day.
The basic structure of the big old house was fine.
However, it needed a tremendous amount of work to make
it an environment in which we felt we could flourish.
While we weren't out to impress anybody with what we
had, each child and adult had definite dreams about what
the house should ultimately be like as a home and a gathering place.

We also wanted to be able to afford the renovations
and redecorating. Does all this sound familiar?

Naturally we had some large challenges, not the least
of which were to keep our value system up front, to keep
contention low, and to stifle foolishness, falseness, selfish-
ness, fatigue, and delusions of grandeur.

We needed to pray. Besides, churches and temples were
dedicated to God, so why not our home? Kneeling around
the master bed, then, we dedicated our home.

My husband was head of our home in a very real and
vital way. He asked each of us to take a turn in these little
dedicatory services. I prayed first. Then in the order of

their birth, each child prayed, expressing his or her feelings and commitment about the new home. Then my husband gave the dedicatory prayer.

It was wonderful. We were of one heart and one mind. The sweet spirit of the Lord filled every soul. And it was amazing to us that in prayer the details of our various expectations became clear to all.

Time passed. This house was never really "finished." There was never time enough nor money enough to refurbish it in the manner we had dreamed of when we moved in and prayed our dreams before God. In fact, our finances got worse instead of better. There were other demanding, diverse trials during these years.

But that day of dedication helped us immeasurably. Through our struggles along the way, we kept referring to the dedicatory prayer when dreams were fresh and spirits humble. We were in these circumstances together from the start, with God, and we pulled together.

That house became our corner of heaven on earth. It was not a showplace, after all. This was the period when missions, weddings, and grandchildren happened. We felt so close to heaven there because we needed God's help often—not to decorate a house but to solve life's problems with eternal reach, according to his will.

A CHILD'S PRAYER

Through adversity we can come to know God, to love him, to value the plan and gift of life, to see his hand in our blessings.

Think of it this way: if we didn't suffer some, if we had everything that we wanted and most of what we needed without asking Heavenly Father, we might drift away from God in our lives. Surely we wouldn't grow in our understanding that we are in debt to the Lord for all our blessings.

It is through adversity and the answers to our prayers that we become a witness to miracles in our time.

Adversity, and the miracles wrought through fervent prayer because of that suffering, is a blessing for people of all ages.

Tippy was the most precious possession in the life of our eight-year-old son. Tippy was a wiggling, lovable puppy with black, curly hair. But unless our son Tony cuddled him, he yapped constantly. He was in a way like a newborn baby. I'd had six children in close marching order, and right then a yapping puppy was not number one on my list of priorities.

But Tony adored Tippy.

One day Tippy disappeared. We searched the neighborhood for him without success. No doubt someone had carried this appealing black bundle off, I explained to Tony, and added that maybe puppies weren't such a good idea on our busy street anyway. I reasoned and comforted and tried to pacify this precious son of ours with his favorite treats. But he would not be changed in his determination to find Tippy.

"Mom, may I say my prayers early today?" he asked when we reached our home again after scouring the streets in our area.

"Of course, Tony. You may pray whenever you like, as often as you like." I was tempted to take this teaching moment to present a discourse on prayer to a ready eight-year-old, but he quickly interrupted me, "Will you come pray with me?"

Together we knelt by his bunk bed. My heart was warm and tender at the little boy's outpourings, but it was fearful, too. What if the puppy couldn't be found, couldn't find its long way home after so short a time with us? Would Tony's faith in Heavenly Father falter?

As it turned out, it was my faith that faltered. My need wasn't as great perhaps. I would have forgotten about that puppy and welcomed the peace from its yapping, except that Tony wouldn't let me. We had an "extra" prayer each day when he came home from school. Each prayer had as its sole purpose the pleading with God to bless the puppy and bring him home safely "someday." Tony was resolute.

Many days passed. One day I sent Tony out to the curb to bring in the trash cans. Moments later he came bounding into the house with the puppy in his arms. Tippy was an emaciated, bedraggled dog with curled fur matted by dried blood. He'd had some terrible adventure. All the way to the veterinarian we cried tears of gladness, and Tony kept repeating over and over, "I knew Heavenly Father would bring Tippy back. I knew it!"

Oh, to be so positive about outcome to prayer! So tireless in waiting for the Lord's timetable.

It was many weeks after this incident that I was giving a talk in a neighboring stake Relief Society. I told about Tippy and Tony's unfailing faith. The next day one of the women in that meeting knocked on my door. She handed me a fat roll of her famous caramel pecan candy. It seems that my story had stirred a memory in her, and she came with candy and a confession. She said she was driving past our home one day near the vacant lot and felt a thump. She didn't stop to check because she just assumed it was a piece of old tire or a stray cat as she saw the black object flip into the tall weeds of the vacant lot. She drove on her way. She was a woman in a hurry to a doctor's appointment.

Tippy had been injured seriously (indeed, the vet confirmed this) and apparently had been recuperating in the field while Tony's prayers were answered, keeping the dog alive. On that last day, Tippy had made his way as far as the trash cans when Tony found him.

In 2 Nephi 26:15 we are promised that "the prayers of the faithful shall be heard." My personal testimony is that this is so.

A HEALING BLESSING

I recall with tenderness and appreciation a time when one of the great General Authorities of the Church placed his hands upon our son when his life was at stake. It was a remarkable experience because of the way that high school boy was prepared to receive what the Lord had in store for him.

We were frightened, I admit. This boy had been longed for and prayed for. At last he was born under special circumstances. Now he was high school age, desperately ill, and we didn't want to lose him so soon. (When is there a time that seems right to have our loved ones die?)

After the anointing with consecrated olive oil by another elder, the General Authority became voice to seal the anointing. He addressed Heavenly Father and explained the desires of our hearts, our love for this boy, our faith before God. This was done to put the sick lad in the right frame of mind to receive the blessing. Then this thoughtful elder addressed our son by name and taught him in an inspired and eloquent manner about the plan of life. He called it the "grand adventure" and suggested that the boy fight to keep his spirit alert to some important learning while the body fought in a frightening experience of life-threatening affliction. He spelled out some of the lessons and heightened the thinking of us all beyond the hospital room, beyond physical restrictions. We were imbued with hope; more than ever the boy wanted to live for a reason, a purpose. Truths had been brought forth that made life all the more precious and worth fighting for. Our son was imbued with a new will to live.

And then the elder shifted the focus in his prayer. He addressed the Lord and spoke of the kingdom of God on earth and the great work to be done among men. Here was a lad being prepared to help in the cause. And the plea went forth to flood the sick boy's mind and spirit with understanding of his part in this important work. A witness was given that the will of the Lord was good enough for this family, this teenager. A witness was made that it was known in this family circle that God lived and loved us and his will for us particularly—whether it be life or death at this time for this son—would be the best in the long view. Then came eloquent words of gratitude for life, for learning experiences and the need for obedience and submission to the laws of heaven, for spiritual growth and comfort, for closeness to God and a part in his plan. It was enough. We waited now upon the Lord.

Our son lived through that grueling, sanctifying trial.

We gained an understanding we would not have had without the dreadful threat to this beloved boy's life. It was the trial before our faith was strengthened—one more time.

God bless the sick and afflicted? He did. He has. He will!

HE WAS WEEPING

It was our custom to kneel in family prayer. In winter, families were secreted together inside, with sounds of the stoker rattling the coal furnace in the basement and the smell of dinner still fragrant. Prayer didn't seem an interruption then. It was a cozy part of the season. Somebody was always sick, too, and the blessings were a valid need.

But in summer, when light still lingered and dogs and children romped in noisy delight on our front lawn, it was different. The voices of the neighborhood kids were a painful distraction, wafting in and out of my consciousness like the furls of a flag in a soft wind, revealing only part of the pattern with each breeze. I'd strain to hear who was already out, what they were saying, which game they were playing while we were still praying. I longed to fly free into the evening cooled by canyon breezes and leave my miserable body there, prostrate over the chair.

We would kneel in the dining room, scene of all formal moments in our family life, each child to a chair so there was less jostling during the prayer. I kept my eyes open until the last moment before the prayer started, studying the hardwood floor marred by an ink spot Junior

258

had made doing his homework, its irregular shape forever on the floor, forever in my mind.

When Daddy prayed it was always longer. He blessed everyone up and down the block by name. Often I couldn't follow what he said because the words were unfamiliar and the style unlike our comfortable conversations. He'd say things like, "Father, we thank thee that all is in accord and that the personnel of this family is complete and accounted for."

Once I visited his office and heard him dictate letters while I waited for a ride up the hot hill. That was it! His prayers were like he was giving dictation. That night when he prayed, I risked the wrath of heaven and sneaked a look at Daddy's face. I was startled. He was weeping! The language he spoke was formal like his letters to important people, but the tears running down his cheeks spoke volumes about the tenderness in his heart.

Daddy loved Heavenly Father so much that he spoke to him in the best language he knew. It was that experience that made me restless with my habitual bedtime routine, "Now I lay me down to sleep. . . ." That summer I ventured a prayer from my heart in my own language instead of reciting something memorized in somebody else's.

CALL UPON THE ELDERS

A violent traffic accident wreaked havoc in the life of a brilliant and beautiful young mother and professional scientist. She went through long weeks of physical and mental suffering. Head injuries had left her with recurring bouts of deep depression. It was a time of confusion and unhappiness for the whole family. She wasn't a member of the Church and didn't know where to look for help. She had attended seminary with friends during junior high school and had lived a clean life, but now her mighty test had come, and she was ill prepared to meet it appropriately. She was besieged by nameless fears and frustrations.

She tried to pray to a God whom she remembered again. But nothing seemed to change much. It was determined that she be given psychiatric help. And, interestingly enough, it was with the psychiatrist that she discussed her restless need for some kind of relationship with Deity. The psychiatrist was an active Church member and finally, at the appropriate point, was able to introduce her to the elders. They reminded her of the restored gospel, which she quickly received. At her hesitant, humble request, through the laying on of hands, she was given a healing, guiding promise.

Did God bless the sick and afflicted woman? Indeed he did! Later she was baptized and confirmed. Filled with joy, she is grateful for the nightmare she had to endure because of what she has learned, what she feels and knows today. The most important blessings of her life she would not have, she says, if she hadn't paid a price through suffering and sought the help of heaven. Today this family is preparing for the temple experience.

It is customary for the person who is afflicted or someone responsible for that person to request the administration of a blessing. The rest is up to the Lord, for he said, "Whatsoever thing ye shall ask the Father in my name, which is good, in faith believing that ye shall receive, behold, it shall be done unto you" (Moroni 7:26).

The late Elder Bruce R. McConkie wrote, "Ordinances of administration with actual healing resulting therefrom are one of the evidences of the divinity of the Lord's work. Where these are, there is God's kingdom, where these are not, there God's kingdom is not. Sincere investigators must necessarily beware of the devil's substitutes of the true ordinances" (*Mormon Doctrine* [Salt Lake City: Bookcraft, 1966], p. 22).

There are times when healing doesn't happen in God's Church. The beautiful thing to remember is that when we seek God's will during a healing blessing, there comes a flood of comfort and peace, as well as the witness of God's love for those involved, even if the person is not healed or the affliction resolved according to desire.

It is important that when we are sick and afflicted, we *think* about calling upon the elders as our special link with Heavenly Father. It is part of God's plan to bolster our own faith, I believe. "And the elders of the church, two or more, shall be called, and shall pray for and lay their hands upon them in my name; and if they die they shall die unto me, and if they live they shall live unto me" (D&C 42:44).

A crushing desire to believe fosters prayer. Reaching out to heaven is really prayer in its most urgent form. It is an effort on our part to be worshipful, to want God to be there! The result of such yearning, yielding, hoping, and reaching can be measured in terms of increased well-being, greater physical buoy-ancy, intellectual awakening, moral vigor, and of joy itself. There also comes a keener understanding of the underlying relationship between God and man and man and man.

MARK'S ANSWER

God bless the sick and afflicted? He does. He will! It is for us to set these holy opportunities in motion.

For example, Lucille had made the brave, long battle with cancer—four years of illness until she reached the terminal stage. The family had endured trauma and trials. In spite of the stress, they had gone about the business of weddings, missions, school activities, and daily chores to keep a family going. Their own illnesses and personal struggles had to be dealt with all the while even as mother's sickness progressed. This meant demanding sacrifice and adjustment. And there was the matter of financial disaster during this period.

Still they loved their valiant wife and mother and were determined to keep her on earth with them. Their prayers pleaded for her life. Their fasting was for her healing. They looked for the miracle still and clung stubbornly to that hope. She was the only woman Mark, her husband, had ever loved, and he simply could not give up Lucille. He couldn't imagine life without her. He wanted *her,* sick or well, but he wanted her alive.

Lucille slipped into a coma, and the doctors knew that the end was nearing. It seemed that only Mark's tenacious faith was holding her here. The strain was telling on him. He sought strength in reading the scriptures and one day read the words in Ether, "Dispute not because ye see not, for ye receive no witness until after the trial of your faith" (12:6).

As Mark sat pondering these things, it happened that one of the elders of the Church came to the hospital room. Lucille had been given administrations along the path of her illness, but as Mark talked with the wise and experienced elder, he felt prompted to ask for a blessing for himself. He wanted the faith and strength to face whatever was according to God's will. Until that moment Mark had thought that what he himself wanted was right and appropriate. A mother and wife belonged with her family until the children were reared, at least! That was what they had unceasingly prayed for over these long years of affliction.

The ordinance proceeded; hands were placed upon his head. As the flow of words went from earth to heaven through an elder of the Church, Mark listened carefully because he was needful. Then, touched by the Spirit, he relaxed; he turned himself over to God, whom he knew afresh lived and cared about him, about Lucille, about their family. As the administration ended, Mark felt a great burden literally lifted—he felt this physically as well as spiritually. Depression eased and anxiety ceased. He knew what he had to do, and he felt right about it, somehow comforted that he was acting in accord with the Lord's purposes.

Mark asked the elder if they now could pray together with Mark being voice. They moved to the bedside of Lucille. Mark knelt there, taking in his hand her fragile, listless one, so dear to him. The tears flowed freely as he prayed, but they were not bitter tears this time. They were a result of the outpouring of a contrite and broken heart. He now had the demeanor of a faithful man who trusted that God would want only the best for his children. Mark prayed for God's will to be done and covenanted that he was willing to obey that will, to let go of Lucille and to trust in divine purposes.

Lucille died only minutes later.

Did God bless the sick and afflicted in that instance? Indeed. Let's follow Mark's story during the years after.

Mark was an example to others suffering similar adversity. Mark was a blessing to a new, younger family whom he gathered in through a second marriage. He and Lucille had had only daughters. Now there were sons to help with his business, sons to teach about the priesthood, sons to prepare for missions and good citizenship. And he was a loving husband to a woman who had been deprived of such joy in her life before. He became a trusted leader in the Church himself and proved compassionate to the sufferers and the strugglers and the questioners because of his personal experience. It is important to realize that the power of God rested upon him because of his obedience and his choice to be on the Lord's side.

Grief must have its day. We have been counseled to weep and mourn for those we have loved well. But let us not forget the value of God's counsel that we seek help as he has provided, that we may get on with life, with our individual mission on earth and not waste time unduly in self-pity or adjustment.

"I WANT EACH ONE TO PRAY"

A specific experience confirmed for me the value in training up a child so that when he is grown he will know the path to follow. Some years ago during a jaunt to St. George the jam-packed car necessitated a few ground rules for our traveling group. Although we were all related, our ages differed greatly, and each came from a separate home. Since we would share a motel room, Great-

grandmother would have a bed to herself; I, the grandmother, would share a bed with my career-girl daughter;
the two scampi preschool boy cousins (my grandsons)
would bed down in sleeping bags in front of the big tele-
vision set.

When we arrived at our room, I suggested a kneeling
prayer around Great-grandmother's bed to dedicate our
temporary home-away-from-home. Each time my own
family had moved over the years we had held a dedicatory
prayer in the new home, that it might be blessed with
God's protection and sweet spirit. I must admit that in this
case, I was also thinking about prayer as a way to forestall
those two destroying angels from turning the place into a
disaster area. It also seemed a golden moment to teach my
grandsons.

We knelt around the bed, and I was voice. Just as I
closed the prayer, three-year-old Jake said, "Wait! Don't
anybody stand up. Now I want each one to pray, and I will
be last." (Had he been taught about priesthood leadership
or what?)

That little child did lead, and we all learned sweet
things from each prayer. When he then insisted on reading the scriptures together out loud, I realized that my
daughter deserved credit for training him well in a valued

tradition. He was even sure there was a Holy Bible in the motel room. Now a young man, Jake still prays and reads the scriptures, but in Spanish, as a returned Guatemalan missionary.

PRINCIPLES
FOR HAPPY DAYS

Remember that the Lord sustains you in your sickness and affliction, in your struggles—not because you are perfect, but because he is.

THOSE WHO SIN DIFFERENTLY

Longfellow wrote that a single conversation across the table with a wise man is better than ten years' study of books.

Henry Eyring was a wise man as well as a world-famous scientist. He was honored by kings, cited by scientific societies, published in professional journals, awarded honorary degrees and titles. He was sought after on the lecture circuit. He had knowledge; he had wisdom; he had an infectious sense of humor that reflected his deep sensitivity to life.

He also walked to work and could outlast jogging companions thirty years younger than he. Dr. Eyring was an interesting and fit man.

To have juggled professional demands and human relationships so successfully makes Dr. Eyring a subject worth our looking into. If we had attended one of his lectures, we would have learned the scope and meaning of the universe and how an atom explodes. His discoveries won him prizes, but his caring brought him friends by the score. Have dinner with Dr. Eyring and you'd learn what makes him a memorable human being. He would talk about you. Then the next time you met, there would be a quick rundown of your family tree, your place of roots, your genealogical connections. Dr. Eyring cared about people.

And Dr. Eyring believed in God.

He was a devoted worker in religious circles, helping people find appropriate directions and valid answers to eternal questions, and encouraging faith when answers weren't yet available. To Dr. Eyring, science and religion were not irreconcilable but were, in fact, mutually supporting when one's understanding had gone far enough. This was the basis of Dr. Eyring's personal philosophy of life: The Lord created the universe with eternal laws; personal relationships to be enriching must be based on eternal principles, too.

On one occasion a group of us were talking about a person we all knew who had a particularly difficult personality problem. Suddenly Dr. Eyring changed the tone of the talk with his comment, "I hope I will always be tolerant of those who sin differently from me."

Oh, Dr. Eyring wasn't talking only about those blatant, cardinal wrongdoings we all try to avoid. He was suggesting the importance of keeping the second great commandment and oft-repeated counsel from God to love each other—imperfect though we might be. And that goes for loving our enemies, too.

"Those who sin differently . . ." what a revelation into a man's motivation! What a secret to the implementation of good relationships in our own lives!

Such an attitude emphasizes the truth that none of us is perfection personified—yet. We need to be patient with ourselves as we work daily at overcoming our weaknesses.

The scriptures remind us of that with the words "continue in patience until ye are perfected" (D&C 67:13). We also will be happier with each other if we develop patience toward others while they struggle with their personal progress, always trying to be tolerant of someone who "sins differently from us."

The inimitable Robert Frost sums it up with these lines from "The Star-Splitter":

> *If one by one we counted people out*
> *For the least sin, it wouldn't take us long*
> *To get so we had no one left to live with,*
> *For to be social is to be forgiving.*

But Dr. Eyring didn't merely *tolerate* others, remember.

He sought to know them better. With knowledge comes understanding, and the miracle of love comes next.

ON THE WAY TO SCHOOL

There was a sight in Taiwan that gave me a dramatic perspective toward agency and accountability.

I was in a village hotel several floors up, leaning out of the window to watch a steady parade of the beautiful children of Taiwan on their way to school. From my vantage point I could see the school some distance away. The children knew the school was there, though they couldn't see it yet, and, of course, they were unaware of my presence.

These dark-haired children were charming in the official school uniform: short navy skirt or pants; clean, starched, white shirt; and on this rainy day, a canary-yellow slicker. Some of the children carelessly dragged their slickers behind them; a few let them fly open; others wore them tightly buttoned, like the whole armor of God.

The path the children were taking through the rice paddy was well trampled, but there were big mud puddles and exciting places to hide between tall rushes.

In a variety of sizes, the youthful army came around

the corner of the hotel—wave after wave of these little people of Heavenly Father's family who lived in Taiwan. *According to their agency,* they dawdled along, were detoured by the slightest distraction, or else pressed toward the mark—the school way up ahead. It was up to them now; parents weren't around.

To watch the children deal with their environment was to see a slice of life in any age group, in any country, at any given time in the history of man.

Some of the children deliberately plowed right through the deep mud puddles time and again, and came forth filthy.

Others automatically marched around the puddles, almost oblivious to them.

Many absolutely could not resist the temptation to gingerly touch a toe in the mire. One little girl, afterwards, stooped over and tried to wipe the mud from her shoe, then from her hand; then she brushed the spot on her clothes where she had wiped her hand, *Mud is tough to erase.*

Life from a window. Agency and accountability. They made their choices, and so do we.

We are like children walking a path in the rain. We can walk in or around the mud of life as we desire, but with our choices come the consequences. And we are rapidly becoming what we are choosing to be for all eternity.

Watch the advance notices. Even you will have to cope with temptation, so keep your eyes open, your answers ready, your resolve strong.

KNOWLEDGE ISN'T ENOUGH

The gospel of Jesus Christ is a wonderful composite of comfort, direction, admonition, and instruction. The gospel provides motivation and impetus for individuals to move forward. Knowing what answers to give in church classes and being able to recite chapter and verse in the scriptures is a great achievement. However, only if a person also actively applies the principles of the gospel to his life is the Lord's plan being fulfilled for the benefit of mankind.

There are two truths to keep in mind.

One, knowledge of the gospel is imperative because people cannot be exalted in ignorance. Whatever intelligence we gain in this life will be part of our being and rise with us in the resurrection (see D&C 130:18).

Two, exaltation depends on our living by the word of God. Wise is the person who will awake and arouse his or her faculties and experiment upon the word, actually applying God's principles to daily living.

Solomon was King David's son. When Solomon became king of all Israel, God appeared to him in the night and asked Solomon what gift he desired. Solomon replied, "Give me now wisdom and knowledge" (2 Chronicles 1:10). Solomon wanted to judge the people fairly and move before them having within himself the power of God, who loves all people.

God gave Solomon wisdom because "thou hast not asked riches, wealth, or honour, nor the life of thine enemies, neither yet hast asked long life; but hast asked wisdom and knowledge for thyself" (2 Chronicles 1:11).

Solomon's experience is a reminder to those called to serve that they should seek wisdom as well as knowledge to make their service indeed beneficial to others. We study, learn, and seek out of the best books, all the while humbly praying for understanding and wisdom. Then, through the power of the Holy Ghost, the heavens will be opened, knowledge will pour down from heaven, and the soul will be greatly enlarged (see D&C 121:45).

Knowledge is not enough for any situation. For example,

people know how babies are made, and still a staggering number of illegitimate infants come into the world. Mistakes are made—knowledge hasn't been enough to forestall problems. Many, many hearts are broken as a result.

People know that eating too much of the wrong foods produces fat in the body. Yet the world is crowded with overweight people who receive shocking news standing on the scales and often suffer the sad consequences of disease and low self-esteem. Knowledge doesn't always control behavior.

People know that dishonesty is against the law of God and the law of the land. But knowledge isn't enough to protect against temptation. Proof of this is in the increasing number of incidents of lying, cheating, robberies, scams, gambling, prostitution, murders, and all manner of situations where people offend and take advantage of others.

Some people may say that they know God lives and that the gospel is true, and yet they persist in ungodlike activity on a greater or lesser scale. Some may listen to the prophet speak but then take issue with his counsel. Some may teach a lesson on faith, but when a loved one dies, they weep and wail and cry, "Why me?"

Knowledge alone doesn't get us into heaven. We need understanding and wisdom, and we need to use them to make life more satisfying for ourselves and others.

SELF-CONTROL

Thomas Jefferson said that nothing gives one person so much advantage over another as to remain always cool and unruffled under all circumstances.

Many have waxed eloquent on this topic. For example, Seneca wrote, "To master oneself is the greatest master."

Aristotle said: "I count him braver who overcomes his desires than him who conquers his enemies; for the hardest victory is the victory over self."

And Browning penned: "When the fight begins within himself, a man's worth something."

"The virtue of all achievement is victory over self," wrote A. J. Cronin. And Edgar A. Guest expressed such thoughts in verse:

> *I have to live with myself, and so*
> *I want to be fit for myself to know;*
> *I want to be able, as days go by,*
> *Always to look myself straight in the eye.*

I don't want to stand with the setting sun
And hate myself for the things I've done.

Everyone gives his life for something, whether it is little or much. Joan of Arc was burned at the stake for her beliefs. We aren't all asked to die the martyr's death by being burned alive like Joan of Arc. Nor are we marched into the lions' den these days because of our convictions. But all of us can be sorely tried at a time when we are challenged, embarrassed, judged unfairly, taunted, ridiculed, or angered. We may find that our principles or needs are quite different from those of our peers. We may need to diet or budget or break some nagging habit. We may need to give up our own interests for the needs of another. Our tempers, patience, or character can be tested smartly even at a change of circumstance. People are mature or immature depending on how they react to what life thrusts upon them; but because we cannot always direct events, we must learn self-control—to govern ourselves. If we fail in responding appropriately to life's challenges, we pay a high price.

The Bible tells us that "as [a man] thinketh in his heart, so is he" (Proverbs 3:27). Another maxim is that acting as though you are, can make you that way. And another is that thinking begets behavior, which begets character. All of these remind us that we ought to do some thinking about what we can take and what we can give and what we can give up. The journey of all the rest of our lives is affected by how we handle ourselves today.

The concept of self-control (or the lack of it) surfaced generations ago. It all began when Eve hearkened to the voice of the tempter and ate the forbidden fruit. She then confessed before God's questionings, "The serpent beguiled me, and I did eat" (Genesis 3:13). Often since then we have been busily blaming someone else or some circumstance for our own weaknesses.

It is true that environment and even heredity have some force in a person's actions and decisions. But always there is the element of choice. Here is a truth that we can lean to—we can be master of our fate. We *can* lose weight, quit swearing, save money, get organized. We can do anything we want to if we want to badly enough.

We can learn to control our attitude about things we can't do anything else about, too.

But there are some things we can do something about, like making it a good day no matter what, and some things we just have to accept and adjust to. And we ought to be making a good day of it with the time we have.

Each of us has his problems, his cross to bear, a lemon

that has been handed him unbidden. Most of us have created some intricacies in our lives by foolish behavior, careless decisions, or thoughtless conversation. We can repent and try harder to understand, to reason through why we reacted as we did. It helps if we look to the lives of others and how they reacted.

Joan of Arc was burned, and tradition has it that she didn't flinch. In 1844 Joseph Smith was shot by a mob in Carthage, Illinois, for his efforts to restore the full teachings of God within a new church. He went, as he said, "like a lamb to the slaughter." Jesus Christ was crucified, and he prayed to God, "Forgive them; for they know not what they do" (Luke 23:34).

These are supreme examples of noble control. As Seneca said, "To master oneself is the greatest master."

I believe this with all my heart. Don't you, really?

Value yourself. As a child of God, hold yourself with such reverence that you are protected against Satan's weapons: temptation, depression, jealousy, anger, self-pity, self-righteousness.

THE OLEANDER

The summer we painted the oleander was the beginning of a lifelong attitude about appropriateness. One doesn't gild the lily. One doesn't tamper with natural beauty.

An oleander in Utah was something of a novelty in those days. Ours was the family treasure. Daddy had invested something of himself in that plant. Some years before, he had packed it in soggy cotton and brought it on the long trip from California to his mother in Salt Lake City. When Grandmother died it was ours, and the more valuable because it had been hers. It was nature, protected. Each winter, ceremoniously, it was swathed in burlap and hauled into the garage. Each time we climbed into the Studebaker it was at the command, "Don't crush the oleander." Each summer it was brought forth to be hosed down, pot-painted, and put in place by the porch. Then at last profuse blooms rewarded everyone.

On this particular day I was suffering—at age three—the tortures of rejection. There was some painting going on at our house, and I had been programmed out. When the supplies were left unguarded, I sought to beautify the oleander. What sport!

What a sense of power I felt changing the look of that shrub with each flamboyant slap of the brush until the shrieks of my parents awakened me to my mischief. It was not beautiful at all. It was ruined, its pitiful petals sticking together in extravagant blueness.

"One cannot improve on God," Daddy declared emphatically, shaking me soundly.

The oleander died, of course, but Daddy's counsel lives in me yet. A chair can be repainted to cover past damage, but a living, growing thing can be spoiled forever through witless tampering. And that goes for people as well as plants.

God's principles are given to help mankind live the
plan with the least heartbreak and greatest success.

WHEN BLESSINGS
TURN INTO BURDENS

Nobody really wants to make trouble for himself or herself. Sometimes, however, that is exactly what we do—we turn blessings into burdens through our actions and attitudes.

Here are eighteen ways we can turn rich blessings into

dreadful burdens. Of course there are other ways, but consider these for a moment.

1. Sin.
2. Don't repent, recoup, or make restitution.
3. Live without prayer.
4. Think you know more than Church leaders—or parents, experts, even God.
5. Be casual about sacred ordinances.
6. Fail to read your patriarchal blessing frequently.
7. Withhold love.
8. Hold a grudge; be unforgiving.
9. Fail to ask forgiveness.
10. Be arrogant, full of pride.
11. Think of yourself first—what's in it for me?
12. Assume that you can get something for nothing.
13. Assume that no one will ever know.
14. Complain.
15. Be ungrateful; count your troubles instead of blessings.
16. Ignore scripture study.
17. Be lazy, manufacturing excuses, ignoring opportunities.

18. Break the Ten Commandments. (Look them over again, just in case you've forgotten the one about the Sabbath day or honoring parents or lying, cheating, adultery, and so on.)

Look to your habits and attitudes. Look to your responses to situations. Don't choose to be a problem. Be a problem solver. Be a burden lifter. Value the word of God and the place of God in your life.

To err is human, but to make unnecessary mistakes in life is not smart. One might even suggest that it is stupid. Surely it can be painful. It is how to turn blessings into burdens.

To take a perfectly good blessing and turn it into a burden through sin or stupidity is courting trouble. One might even call such a course self-imposed adversity. Ignorance of the law or disobedience of fine principles promises problems. And who needs burdens when we could have had blessings?

Consider this simple example: One day I was making a cake to use as a visual aid in a meeting. A committee had a task to perform, and I wanted to show that with proper planning it would be easy—a "piece of cake" as the saying goes.

I arose early and attacked the project with virtuous

enthusiasm. I would make the biggest and best cake I had ever produced—a six-egg cake, light as down and delicious to eat. Just as I began breaking the eggs into the mixture, the telephone rang. The call from the East Coast person in a state of trauma was made according to her time zone and not mine. I listened while I went on with the cake because I was feeling the scrunch of time to finish my visual aid.

It would have been better if I had stopped the mixing altogether. In my concern for the caller, my brain short-circuited. I began tossing egg shells into the mix and eggs into the sink. This fact did not become clear to me until the cake was baked. It was not the lightest cake ever, and there were crunchy shells where one least expected them to be.

I used the cake as a visual aid, all right, but I made a point different from the "piece of cake" idea. I used the cake failure to show how something very nice can become awful when we are not in control, when we don't think through to the result of certain actions, when we don't consider that what we are doing is different from what we ought to be doing, and when what we are doing brings disappointment—even trouble.

A CRUSHING DESIRE TO BELIEVE

Inevitably when affliction hits, doubts seem to crowd the mind. But if you desire to know, if you ache to believe, if you take that first step toward God, he will rush forth to meet you and flood you with proof.

The Lord has challenged us with these words: "Prove me . . . if I will not open you the windows of heaven, and pour you out a blessing, that there shall not be room enough to receive it" (Malachi 3:10).

A blessing so marvelous that there shall not be room enough to receive it? Wonderful! But the question is do you know a blessing when you get one? Or is it true that God's will is hidden by self-will? This may be the very area of faith that needs some working on, some scriptural research, some prayerful pondering, some spiritual mulching, pruning, and feeding, if you will. When the desire to believe in God, to believe that he cares about you particularly, at this moment of affliction, to believe he can bless you according to what is best for you—when that moment comes, it is a kind of "crushing desire to believe" that can bring great peace.

A NEAR-MAGIC
SURVIVAL SYSTEM

1. Count your blessings.

Name the good things God has given you, one by one. In our best moments, each of us can recall times when we have been comforted and strengthened by the Lord and times when our burdens have been eased, if not entirely removed. Let's give credit in such times of remembrance.

2. Keep close to the Lord.

Often it takes a little time before we become converted to a principle, before habits and attitudes change and accommodate a better way. Meanwhile, draw ever closer to the Lord. Mentally, put your hand in his and feel him walking beside you over the rough way.

3. Study the scriptures.

Over and over again we are reminded to find our answers and our direction, our solace and our strength, by scripture study. Why spin wheels in grief or anguish? Just do it! Comfort and ease do come.

4. Be obedient.

Conscientiously apply gospel principles to problem solving and to spiritual survival when you are sick and afflicted. The Lord has said in many ways the thought, "I, the Lord am bound when ye do what I say" (D&C 82:10).

5. Find a way to help others.

Everyone needs to understand this near-magic system for survival. When you learn, teach. When you feel you are a witness to God's goodness, testify of it to others.

Joseph Smith said, 'I teach them correct principles and they govern themselves.' It remains for parents in our day to follow their inspired leaders, especially to see to it that correct principles are taught so that their children have enough knowledge to govern their own decisions.

FINDING VALUE IN A TORN AND TATTERED BOOK

These are the flat facts behind why Jim and I started a Sunday scripture read-aloud even though the children were barely able to read: We knew that our posterity should experience the sweet and saving truths of the gospel for themselves by searching the word with their own senses—seeing, hearing, speaking the word out loud.

We made some personal sacrifice in groceries so that each one had a set of scriptures, except the toddler, who had a *Golden Book of Jesus* from which he took a turn "reading."

It was perhaps the best gift we gave our children through all the years.

Jim introduced us to this tradition by telling us a tender story from his Hawaiian mission days. A worn Bible was his visual aid. In a country town on the island of Maui, a young boy lay close to death with a dangerously high fever. The doctor had done everything he knew. There were no life-saving miracle antibiotics at that time. The elders had been called in to administer a healing blessing. Jim explained to our family, "Before the anointing, I asked the boy if he knew about Jesus. He nodded his head weakly without opening his eyes. Then I put this Bible on his chest and laid his hand on it so he could feel it. I told him this was the sacred book that described all about Jesus and the good things he did—how he placed his hands on sick people and made them well. I read out loud from Mark 9 (we all opened our Bibles to Mark 9), where it is recorded that a father brought his son to Jesus to be healed from a terrible illness. The scripture says: 'Jesus said unto him, If thou canst believe, all things are possible to him that believeth. And straightway the father of the child cried out, and said with tears, Lord, I believe; help thou my unbelief' (Mark 9:23–24).

"I wasn't certain that this sick boy was well enough or trained sufficiently to understand what I was saying," Jim related, "but we went ahead and gave him the anointing and sealing ordinance. When I lifted my hands from his head and reached to take my Bible from his chest, the boy tightened his grip around the book. He would not let it go. And we left.

"Two days later we visited with the family again about the boy's condition. They reported that he was much improved. He had hugged that Bible all night. The family felt sorry that the Bible got soaked from the boy's incredible perspiration as the fever finally broke. But that book became even more valuable to me because of the boy's faith."

Jim flipped the pages to show our children the stained cover and sheets, allowing each child to handle his Bible. It had a profound effect on them.

During every scripture session, each member of our family took a turn reading a few verses from the selected scripture. Not to be left out, the toddler very soberly "read" a brief bit of baby jargon from his picture book. Of course, we flooded him with compliments. Then one day an amazing thing happened. He insisted on reading from my Bible. Apparently he had noticed how the siblings, who were beginning readers, moved a finger across the printed lines. This was to help them keep their place. Sitting on my lap, Tony put his tiny finger on the text in my Bible. When it was his turn to "read," he babbled his nonsense. Suddenly he said, "Jesus!" and pointed to that sacred name in print. Maybe he recognized the letters he had seen in his baby books. Surely something clicked in his mind. Whatever else it was to this child not yet two years old, he miraculously had caught on to reading, which was about symbols the mind recognized to stir the soul. And "Jesus" was his first experience with recognizing truth through the scriptures!

It was a high moment, a memory repeated for our youngest child as he grew up and was ordained a deacon, honored at a missionary farewell, a wedding shower, and then, too soon, a funeral when he was only forty-two and the father of three.

If you have made a mistake and don't correct it,
you are making another mistake.

SOME DON'TS

Here are some familiar don'ts about keeping close to the Lord:

> *Don't forget to prepare your heart to commune with God.*
> *Don't forget to pray.*
> *Don't forget to stay awake while praying.*
> *Don't pray only for favors.*
> *Don't pray for your own way instead of his will.*
> *Don't forget to study the word of God so you will know his will.*
> *Don't forget to listen for the promptings.*
> *Don't forget to repent.*
> *Don't forget to be believing.*
> *Don't forget to perform according to guidance received.*
> *Don't forget to love.*

A CHOICE
GENERATION

Says the little one:
Touch me soft, be gentle
Listen to me, care.
Let me see your eyes so
That I will know you're there.

CELEBRATE YOURSELF

S o what's to celebrate? Check it out. Discover that there are some mighty fine things about being *you*. For instance:

1. Being born, having a crack at life, taking your turn on earth.
2. Being alive today!
3. Being a member of the Lord's "family," being a member of his Church, and having the blessings of leadership, programs, ordinances, and goals prescribed by him.
4. Knowing who you are, why you are here, and where you are going.
5. Counting your blessings—your talents, your particular trials, your family, the place you live, the people you know.

6. With all due respect to everybody else, to all the good and all the struggling souls on earth today—with *all* due respect—you recognize that it is awesome to be one of the young men and young women with a particular purpose.

There are some important things about being *not just ordinary* young men and young women. You see, you are part of a chosen generation. You were born at a certain time so that you could make a special contribution to mankind and play a key position on the Lord's team, if you will. You have been gathered together with a select group from all across the world, fulfilling assignments given to you in the life before this one.

There is more.

You are like other out-of-the-ordinary young men and young women, yet you, yourself, are *unique* among them. You've discovered that being alike but being different offers some interesting challenges. So it will be a great day when you wake up to the reality that there is a system for coping with such challenges. You are on the Lord's side. You have your own heritage, your own hormones, your own gifts, your own childhood conditioning. You have your own particular problems. You have your very special cravings, yearnings, dreams, goals, and—ah, yes—shortcomings. But remember you also have your own testimony that you are a spirit child of Heavenly Father and are known to him. He knows more about you than even your earthly father to whom he assigned you! And both of them love you.

Is that great enough?

Okay, it is summary time. You are somewhat like everybody else on earth—living, breathing, functioning, loving, and getting ready to die someday. You also are like others in your special, chosen group of *not just ordinary* young men and young women in that you have a similar mission here on earth. You know things other teenagers don't—even the really nice ones. You have to be better than just nice. You have to try harder.

You are alike, but you are different. Your preparations for life will include distinguished dimensions.

For the most part, childhood was a piece of cake, wasn't it? Learning to walk, talk, manage toilet training, and then attend kindergarten was slick sledding. But then you stepped across the starting line to adolescence. This is life's most critical period. Now you are experiencing the crucial years, facing the crisis choices. And it's a big happening.

Once you've untied those apron strings and added "teen" after your age number, you learn a screaming fact: It is tough to live in the world but not be *of* it! But hang in there! You'll soon find that there is value in being individual among your own generation—even individual among the rest of the *not just ordinary* young men and young women.

Your innocent view of goodness, peace, safety, easy-come-happiness turns into a mirage. You are assaulted with jarring obscenities, frustrated personalities taking their gripes out on you. The war between good and evil is underway and makes anything going on between nations seem like something out of an old movie. Some of the stuff you learned as a little kid is up for wondering. Life is not fair! All people don't seem to be created equal. Happiness isn't automatic just because you don't smoke or drink. God doesn't touch you with a magic wand on each shoulder to secure your secret desires just because you said your prayers last night. Sinners seem to be having all the fun. Parents have become people you don't know anymore. Nobody understands you, including yourself.

There you are, moving out of childhood with a beautiful burden on your back. You are supposed to grow up wonderful and do your thing. Well, for starters, remember that though you are in a particularly appointed group, you—*you*—are in a class by yourself.

How do you cope with being chosen and being young, with being *not just ordinary* and yet anxious to be *like* and be *liked* by all your friends? You cope by doing good and avoiding evil no matter what! Remember, you can't fool with evil and feel good.

You cope by using your wits, by thinking first and acting afterwards, by continuing to learn truth—getting information to act upon—and by finding out what your specific purpose in life is. But above all, you work at keeping close to Heavenly Father.

For nearly six thousand years God held *you* in reserve to make your appearance in the final days before the Savior comes again to rule and reign on earth. You were born that much closer to that exciting time—later than your parents, your teachers, or the prophets on earth today. The First Presidency stated: "You are not just ordinary young men and women. You are choice spirits who have been held in reserve to come forth in this day when temptations, responsibilities, and opportunities are the very greatest."

Do you know that every other generation before yours has drifted into apostasy? President Ezra Taft Benson taught that ours will not because God has saved for the final inning some of his strongest spirit children, who will help bear off the kingdom triumphantly! "You are a marked generation," President Benson told a group of seminary and institute students in 1987. "There has never been more expected of the faithful in such a short period of time than there is of us. . . . The final outcome is certain—the forces of righteousness will finally win. But what remains to be seen is *where* each of us personally, now and in the future, will stand in this battle—and how tall will we stand?"

Consider the good counsel in this poem, "Character of the Happy Warrior," by William Wordsworth. You see, you are warriors in the battle between good and evil, so find happiness in being, as Wordsworth wrote:

> *More skillful in self-knowledge, even more*
>   *pure,*
> *As tempted more; more able to endure,*
> *As more exposed to suffering and distress;*
> *Thence, also, more alive to tenderness.*

And Emily Dickinson wrote a passionate promise that you should memorize as a good reminder in dismal times:

If I can stop one heart from breaking,
I shall not live in vain;
If I can ease one life the aching,
Or cool one pain,
Or help one fainting robin
Unto his nest again,
I shall not live in vain.

In the booklet *For the Strength of Youth,* a special publication issued by the Church for youth, is the strong plea from the First Presidency of the Church, "We pray that you—the young and rising generation—will keep your bodies and minds clean, free from the contaminations of the world, that you will be fit and pure vessels to bear triumphantly the responsibilities of the kingdom of God in preparation for the second coming of our Savior."

Now, we all agree that you are *not just ordinary* young men and young women. Bonded together in your respective organizations of Young Men and Young Women, you can stand against the conniving, serious mischief-makers walking Satan's path. Legs akimbo and arms locked, you are an awesome phalanx.

Standing tall against evil, you are an impressive group.

YOU ARE A DAUGHTER OF GOD

You have the spark of the divine in you. Whatever you do or don't do won't change this fact. Your spirit was marvelously created in the premortal world by your Heavenly Father and your Heavenly Mother. We don't know much about this, but if you ask in prayer, the Holy Ghost will witness to your spirit of your divine beginnings.

Heavenly Father wants you to succeed and to be happy. He wants you to come home to him after you have lived and learned enough to dwell in his presence.

Marcie was the oldest of ten children. She was twelve when her mother died of cancer. That threw a great load on her shoulders for a time—a lot of around-the-house work, all those children, and a new baby besides. Her dad thought she did a great job. In fact, he was worried about her turning into a Cinderella slave to her family, and so he began looking for another wife to be mother to the family.

When two families mix, adjustments can be difficult for everyone. When the new mother came into Marcie's home, there was trouble at once. She and Marcie didn't hit it off. Marcie's dad couldn't take sides with either one against the other, now could he? It was "push against shove" for Marcie.

Marcie felt that she wasn't valued or loved. She withdrew from the family, struggled with herself, and limped into her fifteenth year in real trouble as a young sinner. New friends hovered around her when she led the pack in thinking up exotic, shameful, and daring things to try.

When she found out that she was going to have a baby, she was heartsick. She knew about babies and the breath of heaven they brought with them to earth. She'd welcomed so many brothers and sisters when Mother was alive. Now here she was bringing one into the world with no home, and she'd hardly had time to be young herself.

Suddenly Marcie needed God again.

Suddenly she wanted him to be there for her. It had been so long since she had prayed. God went out of her life when she withdrew from her family and each night began begging friends to let her "stay over" with them. That's when all the foolishness began.

One day Marcie walked alone up the foothills of the mountains behind her school. She selected a spot to be her Sacred Grove. Then she sat down because somehow she felt self-conscious and silly kneeling. Then she put her arms around her knees, with her head down over them.

Soon her burdens weighed heavy upon her heart, and she began to cry.

She cried for a long time until she was emotionally exhausted. She cried for all that now was going to be and all that never could be again. When at last she grew quiet in body and spirit, she whispered gently toward heaven, "Oh, Heavenly Father, if you are still there, help me! Help me! I'm Marcie, and I am ready for you. Are you ready for me? I'm in a mess, and I have no one. I need someone. I don't know what to do."

Marcie did not see God, as Joseph Smith had done in his Sacred Grove. But Marcie *knew* God in that hour. The Spirit of Heavenly Father flooded over her. Her mind cleared to receive inspiration about what she must do to right her wrong and move forward.

She knew she was loved and known to her Heavenly Father. She knew she would be helped and blessed and forgiven by the Savior. She knew, too, that she could be helped but she had a hard path still to walk. She was thankful that God would be there to help.

You are a daughter of God, and he loves you more than you can ever imagine. Parents truly love their children. Earthly parents still have a lot to learn and may not be able to show love as each child would like it to be shown. But our Heavenly Father is different. He is great, perfect, in charge, and loves you no matter what. Because he abides in the eternal laws according to justice, he has his ways of showing love. Let him! Turn to him.

It made all the difference to Marcie, and it will to you, too.

You see, when you know that you truly are a daughter of God, you understand why the way you live is so critically important and why there are so many people (like me) trying to love, write, teach, preach, and help you make it through life's challenges. That is why the scriptures are full of the good news that God wants you to draw close to him so he can draw close to you.

Sing that song again, sing and believe the words, "I am a child of God . . ." If you are ready for heavier support, you can prove this truth by scripture study and the words of every latter-day prophet on the subject.

Being a child of God means that you are related to Heavenly Father in a special way. And you are loved as a dear family member.

Being a child of God means that you are heir to eternal and divine traits.

Being a child in Heavenly Father's eternal family means

that you should try to live and be like your exemplary parents.

Being a child of God means that you are scheduled to go "home" to heaven someday.

That's the grand plan of life.

YOUTHFUL YOU

L ife is a school and not a reward.

We have to learn how to make our heaven before we can live in it.

This thought might help you here and hereafter:

> *You . . .*
> *make all the difference to . . .*
> *a play*
> *a game*
> *a youth conference*
> *a festival*
> *a church outing*
> *a service project*
> *a fireside*
> *a class party*

By your very presence *you* make all the difference. Everybody really is there. But it isn't just the fact of the more the merrier. It's that *you* add a quality nobody else can. You've already learned to be socially smart and personally responsive. You are interested and caring and enthusiastic and absolutely alive. You realize your responsibility as a guest or a participant to rise to the occasion envisioned by the host or sponsoring committee. Such qualities spell success for a function. But being on the scene isn't really enough. It's being there every moment. Since you are that kind of person, youthful *you* make all the difference.

A PEARL OF A GIRL

Once upon a happy time ago, you were born a daughter. You awakened each day smiling through your yawns. Mother was there, approving of you. Daddy was there, loving you. You were his girl.

God was in his heaven, and all was right in your world.

Then you began to grow. You went from a squishy-legged, dimpled darling to the tooth fairy's best friend. You shifted from "Mother's little helper" to "Mother's pain in the neck" because you borrowed her things, you monopolized the phone, you had homework that could be done only during the dinner hour, and your hair never "worked."

Daddy didn't understand you at all. You had traded sitting on his lap for spending time with *that* boy, and Daddy hoped you didn't sit on *that* lap! And you sulked a lot.

You couldn't understand yourself for a lot of years. Daddy called you "Princess," and you felt like one (except when your hair didn't "work," which was much of the time). In front of your own bedroom mirror you had real possibilities—which quickly vanished on your way to school.

How to win control of yourself? How to be what you want to be? How to know what you want to be? How to make your hair "work"? How to be a pearl of a girl? A pearl of a girl all the way up the age ladder, too.

For starters, you begin where you are, use what you have to work with, and move steadily in the direction of your field of dreams. You expect delightful surprises.

Get organized. Make lists. Set goals. Sort and sift and select on the basis of *your* life. Recite: "To every thing there is a season. . . ." Check it out in Ecclesiastes 3—that scripture says it all, doesn't it?

You make value judgments all along the way, learning what to take hold of and what to cast aside; when to control and when to submit; when to steal the scene and when to boost the ego of someone else.

You have your belief system programmed in. You benefit by the positives—you are a child of God, your life has a purpose, there is a "Super Plan," and someone watches over you and wants you to make it. Your life's tests will be different from someone else's. So will your strengths. (But what if every tennis match ends in 6–0, 6–0 for the other player? At least you don't trip yourself up at the game of life.)

No way, absolutely no way, will you allow yourself to hang out in the dark corners of negativism. Catch yourself in *that* act and you'll stomp on statements like "I can't," "I'm afraid," "It's too hard," "I'm not good enough." Shout out, "I can try!"

And you keep on growing. You keep pace with what is happening with programs for *not just ordinary* young women. You keep matching your disappointments against your successes.

You study and pray and experiment on the word to

increase your faith. Faith is at your core. The Light of Christ is the center of your being.

You stand for truth and goodness, fairness and agency for all people.

You begin to understand how great is the worth of the human soul.

You witness the inevitability of sowing and harvesting, cause and effect, choices and accountability.

You have a life, and you can change. You have a mission, and you can be constant. Your feet are on the ground, but your reach is for heaven.

And you love, love, love Mom and Dad and the siblings; the dear old man on a walker down the block; the Young Women leader who coaxes you through the system; the tutor for your college exams; and Heavenly Father, who hears and answers your prayers, whose Spirit quickens yours.

Now, listen to a prophet's voice: "I hope our young women of the Church will establish early in their lives a habit of Christian service. When we help other people with their problems, it puts ours in fresh perspective. We encourage the sisters of the Church—young and older— to be 'anxiously engaged' in quiet acts of service for friends and neighbors."

The way to become a pearl of a girl is to remember who you really are. Keep yourself clean inside and out. Keep yourself healthy, and work to be wise—learn God's lessons.

Fix yourself up pretty as can be, shining from crown to soles. Modulate your voice to match your facial expression. Your face, you know, reveals what is inside you— nice, naughty, or vain. And the face you have when you are forty is exactly what you deserve, I've always said. (Oh yes, you'll grow up to at least turn forty—hopefully!)

Eat well, sleep only enough, hustle your homework, and help with the housework. Get good ideas for good times. Train your ears to hear, your eyes to truly see, and your heart to pound with caring.

Be glad you are you, not another instead. It isn't how tall or how small you turn out to be; it's what you are inside that counts.

Girls, as women yours is the gift to love, to influence for good. Get those young men to go on missions. Insist on clean language and clean topics of conversation from them so that they are as careful to avoid swearing and gossiping as you are. (You are, aren't you?) Your gift of love should extend to older people and to the little folks you tend. It should extend to teachers at church and parents at home. Find appropriate ways to be kind to all who cross your path. I know a group of young women who all decided to wear striped T-shirts on the same day to school. They got the word around to all the girls in their crowd—except one, who was not absolutely killingly cute and popular! Their trick worked, of course. Yes, she was crushed, felt out of it, cried at home, and hated to go back to school the next day. How would you feel?

Think before you break a heart—even halfway.

You have megabytes to burn. Think about this idea: Imagine a great factory where little or no work is done: buildings that cover acres, miles on miles of corridors, rooms after rooms, machines of a hundred different kinds. Every known scientific device, every known scientific principle in usable form is embodied in one room or another; there is equipment more perfect than anything ever before dreamed of. But that whole great plant, with all its possibilities, all its intricate mechanism, is standing idle, not abandoned, but not kept up. Only the footfalls of watchmen echo along the empty corridors; cobwebs are across the windows, around the doorknobs, between the spokes of the great flywheels, and thick dust over everything. The delicately adjusted machinery is motionless, rusting silently away; the whole wonderful plant, with all its marvelous equipment, practically going to waste.

What is it?

That's a leading psychologist's idea of the average human mind. But since you are anything but average, start burning those megabytes in the program of the Lord to move you toward your highest possibility.

SOMEDAY

Someday, sooner or later, somebody is going to offer you a drink. Somebody will coax you to try a cigarette. Somebody will taunt you to get stoned. Somebody will jeer until you step up the car speed or step down to his moral level. Somebody will plead for an answer from you during exams. And somebody just might scoff at your devotion to God.

And what are you going to do about it?

Emerson said, "It is easy in the world to live after the world's opinion; it is easy in solitude to live after our own. But the great man is he who in the midst of the crowd keeps with perfect sweetness the independence of solitude."

How can you withstand the social pressures that go against the grain of your special life?

Make up your mind ahead of time. Consider *why* you have the standards you do.

Have ready answers: Clever, interesting, fun but firm things to reply when given an offer to lower your standards in any way.

Act with confidence. You may be nervous or embarrassed or even frightened, but don't let it show.

Change the subject. Refuse to take such a foolish offer seriously. Quickly move on to another subject.

Having done all . . . *stand. Withstand!*

No matter how much you are teased, tempted, taunted, coaxed, laughed at, or pleaded with, remember who you are and what you want for your own life.

SATISFACTION GUARANTEED

There was a boy whose room was the local disaster area in the house. Before self-destruct time happened, his mother took a stand. In the doorway she stood like a five-foot-four giant colossus, and her words sounded as if she meant what she said.

"Son, you and I have a problem."

"Oh? What is that?"

"Your room couldn't even pass for a yard sale."

"That bad, huh?"

"That bad, Son."

"Well, Mom, did you want to have a garage sale?"

"No, sweetness, I do not want to have a garage sale. I want you to clean your room—like new."

"Well, it's my room, so forget it."

"Well, it's my house and I can't forget it."

"So that's the problem?"

"You got it! Now, clean up your room—FAX-fast."

"But Mom, I am only one person."

"Who would ever believe that? There are enough socks under that bed to—"

"Yeah, yeah—to clothe an army."

"You have heard that before."

"Right."

"You will not hear it again. The next thing you hear will be the sound of your guitar crashing against your head."

"Mother! I am shocked!"

"I am, too, by the sight of your room. Use your agency and get this place safe."

"Agency?"

"Agency."

"What does that have to do with socks under the bed?"

"Just this—you choose to live like a pig and you get to live with the—"

"Relax, Mom. I am way ahead of you. This cluttered room is already history."

"Son, you are not just an ordinary boy. I am thankful for you and that you get the picture. I expect satisfaction guaranteed—in the room cleanup and with all the rest of your life."

This boy was right, in his way. He was only one. And so are you, but this is your stretch of the turf, your time to sing your song. What you do with your time, what you choose to become, includes, of course, keeping your quarters clean, but this is only the beginning.

You know that this stage of life, with the challenges that you face and the expectations adults have for you, is only the beginning. Today, the very wise say, is the first day of all the rest of your life. Whatever it is to be is up to you. Fortify yourself and go for the altogether prize. Pray, prepare to live well and contribute much, and perform—do it!

Consider these lines from e. e. cummings: "To be nobody-but-yourself—in a world which is doing its best, night and day, to make you everybody else—means to fight the hardest battle which any human being can fight; and never stop fighting."

That's it. The rewards are awesome, and the satisfaction is guaranteed—if only you'll continue to grow up wonderful.

CHOOSE TO STAY CHOICE

You are part of a choice generation—the generation born that much closer to the second coming of Christ:

Trained up in the way you should go by new methods to help you learn better, faster.

Owner of more personal property and equipment (electronic and sports) than any generation before you.

Aware of the real meaning of the brotherhood of man.

Tolerant and accepting of people who are different from you in belief, in nationality, in political thinking, in economic or educational opportunities.

Groomed and bred by the best in health care.

You are self-starting and ambitious to improve. You invest your humanity informally, grandly or simply as the situation demands. And you study. College entrance being competitive these days, grades and qualifying have a big place in your life.

So there you are—intelligent, beautiful, studious, spiritual, tolerant, socially smart. There is another area for which to applaud you—you believe. God is part of your life. Your faith is less blind than your parents' faith. Your life hasn't been so sheltered, and you make your choices out of comparison, with knowledge, with confidence. As a result, you understand more about repentance than past generations your age. You do what is right not just out of duty or obedience but because you've considered the alternative.

Many young people in the world today aren't blessed with your kind of understanding about life. They don't understand about life before this and life after this and how life now fits in between. They think they invented agency and attitudes about overpopulation and personal rights. They think they are the only ones who abhor war, and yet they'll tolerate violence on the streets.

You are a choice generation because of your timing in the scheme of things, but never forget that your own agency to choose, to act, to resist, to contribute, has a great deal to do with your being noteworthy, too.

So, choose to stay choice.

A TRIBUTE TO YOUTH

Some people insist upon stating what's wrong with today's youth. But actually there is much that is right with you. You get higher grades, go to church more, eat fewer sweets, serve better, travel farther, think more deeply, have firm opinions of your own, know more about your country and current affairs, spend more and shop better, play more but study more, too, than your counterparts of other years.

You are on-the-go, creative, tongue-in-cheek creatures who delight in unnerving parents and commitments to an unfamiliar cause. But beneath an appearance that may be shocking to adults, there are hearts searching for the good, for truth, for values that rest well on the conscience.

Yours is a grown-up generation, one to be reckoned with. You earn higher wages and boast more talent skills than any other age-group in history. A small percentage of you are termed "delinquent" and often color the case for all the parents. But the remaining may go quietly along preparing to take the torch for our tomorrows.

GIVE ME FIVE!

FIVE SENSELESS SINS

"'For all that, let me tell you, brother Panza,' said Don Quixote, 'that there is not recollection to which time does not put an end, and no pain which death does not remove.'

"'And what greater misfortune can there be,' replied Panza, 'than one that must wait for time to end it and death to remove it?'"

In other words, your worst mistakes, your wildest nightmares won't disappear with the dawn. Better to avoid such trouble in the first place.

Here are five foolish mistakes, five stupid moves, five senseless sins that can ruin your life, as well as your sleep.

1. Believing that everybody is doing it. It's a fact that everybody is *not* doing it. You aren't, for example. Of course, the worldly-minded will attempt to get you off your pedestal to "do it"—whatever "it" is. It can be the beginning of trouble for you if you heed the howl of the witless herd and give in. Even if it seems that a lot of people are doing something that is physically, mentally, legally, or spiritually abusive, you had better stay away from such decisions. Numbers have never made a wrong right. Stupid sin, which amounts to self-destruction, is not for you.

2. Assuming that your generation invented sex, drugs, and speed on the highway. Can you hear the familiar cry? "But things are different now!" No, they are not that different. Adam and Eve knew about sex before you were thought of. Cain killed Abel not too many years into man's recorded history. People have always had the same temptations that you have today (they come under different labels now, that's all), and you have the same commandments that other people have had throughout the generations.

3. Forgetting who you are. You are not like everybody

323

else. You have walked in holy places. You have had hands placed upon your head for blessings from God. You may forget a lot of things—your mother's birthday or your Social Security number—but don't forget who you are and what your goals are. All eternity is at stake. Would you be so foolish as to plan on a university education and then go ahead and crash your grades in high school?

4. *Lying to your bishop.* Never lie to your bishop. You can't get away with it in the long haul. He's inspired and called by God to watch over the people of your ward. The Holy Ghost lets him know if your are telling the truth or not. Don't lie to your parents, either. That goes hand in hand with the mistaken notion that grown-ups don't understand or can't remember or should mind their own business. It is far better to work at avoiding sin than to multiply ways of covering it up.

5. *Refusing to recognize truth.* Ignoring the symptoms. Passing over the fruits of obedience. Going the way of the world. Refusing counsel. Dishonoring your parents. Quitting the business of personal prayer. Blowing your one chance to live. This is heavy stuff here. Watch yourself. Be honest with yourself. Keep in mind the idea that even bank robberies are spawned in someone who probably started with doing something like stealing pennies.

FIVE GOOD MOVES

It has been said, "The evil that men do lives after them." On the other hand, it can also be said the good that men do lives after them. Try that out in life! Jesus lived two thousand years ago in a remote corner of the earth—but what a following! To become like the Savior a person has to do more than slap somebody's palm!

Here are five good moves, five shining moments, five wonderful ways to make life better.

1. Improve the shining moments. One chance to live, and it is the season to be young. Make every moment better than you expected—like the times with your friends, the talks with your parents, the performance with your musical group, the meetings at youth conference, the wonder of winning a game, the gratitude for a prayer answered. Improving and reaching should be almost beyond your grasp—"else what's a heaven for?" asked the poet. A moment becomes shining when you perform beyond your natural ability—just as if you were God-blessed!

2. Thank God you are blessed. You are *not just* an *ordinary* young man or young woman; you are God-blessed. If ever an identity crisis occurs in your life or your self-worth sags, claim your blessings. Ask and it *shall* be given . . . you! You may have to work through some tough times, rotten relationships, ugly temptations, searing sicknesses, but you will be blessed with strength to endure, to overcome, to find joy. And that's the truth. Repeat after me, and then twenty times more, "I am loved—no matter what, God loves me." Then feel the healing happen.

3. *Keep growing in the gospel.* Someone once said something like, "A lot of people are just religious enough to be miserable: they can't be happy at a wild party, and they feel uncomfortable at testimony meeting." But not you. The more you learn through precept and prayer about the gospel and God, the more comfortable you feel on your knees, in the chapel, in the midst of the world. It's a shining moment indeed when you feel the grace of God wrap around you like a fleece blanket. With God, nothing is impossible.

4. *Dream a great dream.* Make your part of the world a kinder, gentler place. Dream a great dream of being a people pleaser instead of a problem person. You can do things nobody else can do. You might be the one to strive for the Olympic gold and set a brave example by comforting the losers. You might be the one to wheel your mom around and be her legs for errands. You might be the one to make friends with a new foreign student at school who is laughed at. One such girl had an ice-cream cone thrown

in her locker at school by guys who stood by waiting for the chance. A younger student put her arm around the girl, offered to help her clean up the mess and to walk home from school with her. Let your enthusiasm (which means something like "God in you") show. It's contagious.

5. *Learn.* Learn how to say no and make it stick. Learn from the mistakes of others, such as people in the scriptures, celebrity press, family members, and friends. When you and your mom were the world, she told you about burning your fingers on hot stoves, didn't she? Learn from what those in authority over you *now* have to teach. Learn what is truth and what is trend. Learn which truths are critical (it is true that an egg cooks in boiled water, but that's not as important as knowing the true reason behind chastity). Learn which trends are fun and which are cheapening or even dangerous.

When you plant a tree, you will remove about twenty-five pounds of carbon dioxide from the air every year. Too much carbon dioxide is a culprit, so you are an environmental helper. When you plant a seed in someone's heart that you know that Jesus lives, loves us, and has a plan that works for the happy life—when you plant *that* seed, you've changed people.

TALK IT OVER

If talking to your plants works magic, try talking to your parents! In the right time and in the right way such communication can bring desired results.

There is a right time, a better time for everything, including asking for money, getting permission, issuing a complaint, talking things over. Putting it to your parents squarely, you may get some straight answers to some tough questions.

Or you may get a lecture, an awkward silence, a desperate attempt at changing the subject. You may not like what you hear. You may refuse to listen.

Impasse. Nowhere. Frustration for everyone.

The generation gap in action.

But keep trying. You're involved here with people who care, who love you—anyway. A sincere grown-up-to-grown-up approach in facing the problems of life can be beneficial to all concerned. Each side of the generation picture tries a little harder to wear the other's glasses. Each assumes the other is a well-meaning, intelligent child of God. Each approaches the task of arriving at agreement on disagreeable subjects with an attitude of appreciation for all the other one is trying to be, for all he really is.

Dad's knowledge and Mother's understanding can be powerful helps in the mean wrestle with life. Your fresh learning, positive approach, and simple faith give valuable perspective.

We hear some stern admonishments that youth should "honour thy father and thy mother." What we don't hear often enough and understand fully is the importance of the rest of that scripture: "that thy days may be long upon the land which the Lord thy God giveth thee" (Exodus 20:12).

ANGELS
AND MIRACLES

Angel stories confirm God's existence, prove God's power, underscore his love for us, and emphasize his mission to bring to pass the immortality and eternal life of everyone. It is for us to keep faithful so that we may be in a position to receive such unspeakable joy as he has in store for us.

ANGELS AND PEACEABLE THINGS

God's angels are a thrilling study. Clearly, angels get around. They have mingled with the very elect in heaven and on earth. They have been on a first-name basis with the prophets and patriarchs recorded in the stick of Judah and the stick of Joseph. They have dealt with kings and rulers of exotic lands and with anxiously engaged heroes and heroines of the Reformation and Restoration. But angels also have touched the humble among mortals. The scriptures affirm they have formed innumerable concourses between heaven and earth. Angels have been spectators to the world's vibrant moments and have participated in one way or another in the grandest—and the quietest—events along a course from the War in Heaven to the Garden of Eden; through the scattering of family tribes and covenant children; through the birth, trials, mission, crucifixion, and subsequent resurrection of Christ; and on to the season of joy with the early Saints of the Restoration of the fulness of the gospel. . . .

How blessed we are by Heavenly Father and the Lord

Jesus Christ and the peaceable things of their kingdom! So much the better if learning the truth about angels both delights us and awakens us to God's sacred gift of angels in our midst, for, as Moroni said, "Neither have angels ceased to minister unto the children of men" (Moroni 7:29).

Moroni should know.

When we are in trouble and are reassured that God lives and is aware of our tragedy—especially through sending angels to help—life's trials are not only more endurable but also tinged with unsuspected blessings and purpose.

"ALMOST!"

The following story is shared by Laura, who had a sister Elise, a young mother who had suffered greatly in her few years of marriage to an abusive husband who at last had been restrained by law to keep away from her. Through it all Elise had remained true and faithful as a leader of youth, until she finally failed fast to a mystery virus. When the following incident occurred, she lay near death in the hospital. Laura described the sacred experience:

"I had gone to visit Elise in the cardiac intensive care unit. She was very fragile and restless. However, she greeted me with her usual warmth and charm, calling me by name. She beckoned me close to her and whispered that there had been people surrounding her bed who wanted her, she said. 'There are people here—pushing me—they've come to get me to take me on a trip from which I will never return.' She confessed to me that she had argued with them, but when I came in they had gone away. Then she asked me to pray with her for peace from this feeling of darkness. The prayer was short, but we were blessed with a wonderful outpouring of the Spirit. I sat in a chair close to her bed, and we both dozed for a brief time. Suddenly I was startled by the sound of her voice. She was talking to someone else, absolutely oblivious of me.

"The spirit in the room was wonderfully enveloping. Elise was looking up toward the ceiling. Her face was radiant. It had changed—this attractive young mother who had been so ill now was extraordinarily beautiful, full of light and love. Her eyes were shining and her smile soft and sweet and wholesome as she talked earnestly to someone I couldn't see or hear. I could hear only her voice, but clearly she could see and hear her invisible-to-me visitor. Her conversation was appropriately paced, and from her response I perceived that she was needed in heaven and that her children on earth would be all right. She had struck a bargain with heaven for a little more time to get her family affairs in order.

"I stood there quietly watching until she closed her eyes and relaxed in bed. I asked, 'Elise, honey, were you talking with the Lord?' She turned toward me and answered brightly, 'Almost!' Nothing more was ever said about this. She died in a couple of months, prepared to move on. As for myself, I felt gratitude for being allowed to witness such a lovely connection with heaven when Elise talked to her angel."

AN ANGEL HOVERING OVER US

Janna is a young mother in whom I am interested because of her talent, goodness, and the way she responds to life. Surely others learning of the experience she had with her baby, Emma, will be inspired.

"In the mornings I typically bring the baby into the

bathroom with me and sit her in her bouncy chair on the floor next to me as I get ready for the day. This way, I can talk to her and keep her relatively happy during the short time it takes to make myself look as presentable as a tired, new mom can look.

"One day, when she was about two months old, we were following this routine when the light fixture came crashing down from the ceiling. Glass shattered in all directions as the fixture hit the floor. Several pieces flew into my bare feet.

"It took me a moment to figure out what had happened, and fortunately I thought quickly enough to avoid stepping on the glass as I instantly headed toward the baby, who, remarkably, wasn't crying at all. *How is it possible that she wasn't hit?* I thought when I heard the silence. But she was fine. My tears were enough to make up for hers as I picked her up and inspected every inch of her small frame. Glass was everywhere—under her chair, behind her chair, next to her chair, even on her chair. But her soft skin and bright eyes were untouched. At this point I started to feel the pain in my own feet and looked down to see that they were bleeding quite a bit. Then suddenly I was overcome with the warmest, most comforting feeling. The thought then entered my head that Emma's guardian angel had been hovering over her chair, protecting her from this freak accident. It was the same feeling I had had as I spent the last part of my pregnancy in bed, thinking about the tiny child I was carrying inside me. I knew then that angels were watching over her and me. She was born as healthy and perfect as any baby. After this accident I again felt that the Lord had seen fit to let me know that this child was special, someone whom I needed to rear and teach in such a way that she might grow up to fulfill her own divine purpose on this earth."

Angels in our midst confirm God's existence
and underscore his love for each of us.
Our challenge is to keep faithful so that we may
be in a position for the further and unspeakable
joy that he has promised.

TO BE KNOWN BY GOD

The incident that Mark Pehrson shared with me happened when he was driving his wife and another couple home from a dinner party. "It was just one of those things, you know?" said Mark soberly. "Road construction at a main intersection, traffic lights improperly timed to accommodate traffic flow, a driver racing through a yellow light and smashing into our car. Diane's side of the car received the brunt of the broadside hit. The impact was so horrendous that it knocked the car five hundred feet from the street into a vacant parking lot behind an empty commercial building. It was totally dark and quiet after the screeching noise of the crash.

"My first thought was for Diane. 'Are you all right, honey?' I asked, wiping the blood from my eyes with my coat sleeve, and twisting to look at her. Suddenly there was a light about her—the lights were out on the car, and there were no lights on in the old parking lot, *but she had light about her face!* As I stared at her, waiting for an answer, the light became increasingly brighter until she really glowed. She had this beautiful smile, and her face looked so peaceful. It was then I realized that she was gone. But there was something else—she was not alone. The car seemed crowded with personages about her. I felt them there. And there was echoing stillness, not empty silence. It was incredibly sweet. Though I wept for the loss of her companionship, which I had enjoyed for many years, I was so grateful for this spiritual manifestation of angels. I knew that this had been no accident, but it had been God's will.

How wonderful to be *known by God* that way! I knew that Diane was all right, and I would be too." Mark and Diane's children and grandchildren treasure this witness.

The night of the accident, Mark and Diane Pehrson had been returning from dinner at the oceanfront home of Alice, a lifelong friend. That spring day Alice had gathered blooming succulents from a hill near her home to decorate the dinner table. Now each spring when those blooms reappear and turn the field into a purple and white tapestry, Alice sits on the hill thinking of Diane and weeping— marveling, too, at the wondrous ways of God. She said: "He gives us joyful relationships, exquisite beauty of nature, comfort, and evidence that heaven is close. What Mark saw and felt when Diane was caught up to heaven is, I feel, sacred as well as a true witness to me."

HEAVENLY HELP

The following story is about a young mother who, like most of us, wasn't perfect but surely wanted to keep on the close side of God.

Margaret was a caregiver to Joe, her invalid husband. She also had young children to provide for. She cursed the storm that delayed her getting home from work on time to pull her materials together, check on the children, and take off for a university forty-five miles away. She had a lecture to give. One more delay that really soured her mood was trying to roust her sons to get the walks shoveled before dark. She had screamed at them, lost her cool entirely—too much pressure, too heavy a load. But she *had* to work! She didn't need that kind of guilt on a night like this.

"Rats!" she exploded as the blinding storm delayed traffic. This snow was serious snowman quality, she thought to herself, as she negotiated the on-ramp and began progressing across the lanes of traffic to the far left lane so that she could pick up her route south at the interchange up ahead. She had driven this stretch countless times; it was just that with the snow screen it was like trying to do it blind! She counted: first lane, second lane, third lane—or was it just the second lane? She couldn't see, and she'd lost track. What if something happened to her on a night like this, feeling as she did about dumping on the boys at home? A silent but specific prayer swelled her heart, "Father, forgive me. Forgive me, please. Take care of Joe and my boys. Help me to get back safely to them. I need a chance to make it up to them. Oh, Father! We need each other, and I need thee. Help me, help me."

Now her snow-clouded vision was watered by tears. Confused, Margaret flipped her blinker to signal left and moved into the passing lane. At once she realized her mistake. She had gone too far! Obviously she had already been in the passing lane and was headed down the slope into the median strip.

"Oh, God, my Eternal Father," she cried out loud. Just then she felt another power wrest the wheel from her hands, and with a strength she had never had, the car was turned sharply back up the slope, through the slush and snow to the passing lane, which was miraculously free of traffic at that very moment!

Margaret was safely on her way again, trembling all over though she was. Over and over again she spoke out loud to give thanks for an answered prayer. She felt protected all the way to the university.

By the time she stood in front of her class, she was mellowed. She did not tell them about her close call, nor did she try to describe her feeling about what had happened to her. She knew it was heavenly help. She hadn't *seen* anything, but that it was an angel helping her was confirmed by the tenderness of spirit that overwhelmed her through the power of the Holy Ghost.

HAPPY BIRTHDAY

Angels are in our midst in many ways. The story of Peggy and Jarvis shows how angels can keep someone from self-destruction. Peggy and Jarvis each came from a good heritage and tried to live according to gospel principles. Of course, like the rest of us, they were not perfect—but they wanted to be. They had fallen in love, married, and then had three children in stair-step style. Then came the twins. They brought hearts full of joy to their parents, but what a challenge! The struggle was financial as well as emotional and physical for two people learning to live together in love.

Then Jarvis accepted a sales job with immediate financial benefits, and they felt on top of all happiness. However, the job required that Jarvis travel nearly twenty-five days out of every month. Peggy began to wear down from the burden of being, practically speaking, a single parent. Besides, she had a garden to keep and an enormous laundry and household chore schedule, and she helped out at church.

One day Peggy reached her lowest ebb.

It was her birthday. Jarvis was out of town, of course. How would she celebrate? Bitterly she thought about it. "Oh, I know, I will celebrate by painting the nursery." Jarvis had put it off since the promise he made to her when the twins were born. Well, she'd show him! Peggy climbed a ladder, bitterly singing, "Happy birthday to you, Peggy," and began splashing on paint to the tune of self-pity. The more this went on, the more destructive her thinking became. She thought about plans for *bolting this trap.* She seriously considered hiring a sitter for the children and simply escaping with a new identity. The thought of leaving the twin babies brought forth fresh sobbing. But now she cried because she was ashamed; next she cried out to God for help. Suddenly, she felt warm arms of love encircle her. She gasped, thinking Jarvis had surprised her by coming home and had climbed the ladder below her to hug her. She turned her head to greet him and saw nothing, though she till felt the warm hug that comforted her. She knew that God had heard her prayers, and she was strengthened beyond any expectation.

What angels do is often well disguised, but may it suffice to say that God is there for us, and his angels stand by to do his bidding.

GOD CREATED ANGELS

God created angels. We do not comprehend exactly how he did so, but with God nothing is impossible— all things have a wise and holy purpose. The truth about angels, for example, is wonderful to consider and in keeping with the Lord's self-explained mission: "For behold, this is my work and my glory—to bring to pass the immortality and eternal life of man" (Moses 1:39). Let there be no doubt: God created angels, and he sends angels for the good of mankind.

The work of angels reflects their individuality and preparation; God knows well how and when they can serve best. This is also true of us mortals. Not all of us have the same gifts, nor can they be of the same use to Deity and mankind. One can teach the word, another is given exceedingly great faith to heal; another is compassionate, another merciful; another has expertise in righting wrongs, in scientific advancement, in creating beauty.

Some have the gift of "the beholding of angels and ministering spirits" (Moroni 10:14).

A COMMAND TO REPENT

Amazing help comes to people important to God's
purposes today. The woman who figures in the following incident told me her story personally and gave permission for my use of it to help other people, so long as
she remained anonymous. We will call her Adelaide.

Adelaide had a spiritual experience in order to bring
about a necessary repentance on her part. At the time of
the incident, she was the wife of a newly called Church
leader who was also an important figure in the community
and financially successful. She had lived a very worldly
social life in keeping with their position. When her husband received the Church call, he worried because
Adelaide was not totally sincere in her efforts to conform
to Church standards. He was patient and loved her deeply,
though her values proved embarrassing on occasion.
Repeatedly and earnestly he prayed for strength and for
her repentance. He was certain that his own efforts to

serve the Lord were rendered ineffective because of her compromising example.

One Sunday he was speaking from the pulpit, and Adelaide was seated at the end of a pew on the right side of the aisle in the chapel. While her husband was speaking, she heard her name called. It came from the aisle into her left ear. Automatically she turned toward the sound but couldn't see anyone. The same thing happened again, and she turned to the people behind her, who were oblivious to what she was experiencing. A third time the voice called out, again addressing her by name. Annoyed, Adelaide said to herself, *What is going on here? What in the world is this all about?* Then her heart began to pound. She felt a new energy, and she heard these words, "Adelaide, support thou my servant Herbert in his important calling. Prepare your life that you may be a proper helpmeet for him in his work in the kingdom of God."

Adelaide was thunderstruck and frightened. She bowed her head in shame and humility as she felt a gentle brush across her shoulders. Amazed that heaven had noted her problem, she later told me, "An angel had touched me, and I found the courage to do what I had to do." She changed her life and found joy in supporting her husband and being obedient to God's commands.

We may not always *see* angels, but their presence can be felt or a voice heard that is lifting and helpful. . . .

Angels do not pop on the scene or fly through the heavens simply to please mankind. They do God's will in the serious pursuit of helping to bring about the fruits of the atonement of Christ. They combat the forces or followers of Satan.

REFERENCES

Marriage and Family

"An Eggbeater in the Silver Chest?" from *Life—One to a Customer* (Salt Lake City: Bookcraft, 1981), pp. 125–27.

"What Is a Family?" from *Life—One to a Customer* (Salt Lake City: Bookcraft, 1981), pp. 118–20.

"A Turning Point," from "The Lord's Errand," in *Turning Points*, comp. Vaughn J. Featherstone (Salt Lake City: Bookcraft, 1981), pp. 9–11.

"True Beauty," from *Sunshine for the Latter-day Saint Soul* (Salt Lake City: Bookcraft, 1998), pp. 9–10.

"The Blessings of Marriage," from *Count Your Many Blessings* (Salt Lake City: Bookcraft, 1995), pp. 80–81.

"Beginning the World All Over Again," from *Life—One to a Customer* (Salt Lake City: Bookcraft, 1981), pp. 43–46.

"A Necklace for Mom," from *Merry, Merry Christmases* (Salt Lake City: Bookcraft, 1988), pp. 40–43.

"Tradition," from *Merry, Merry Christmases* (Salt Lake City: Bookcraft, 1988), pp. 43–45.

"'Mama, You've Got Trouble,'" from *God Bless the Sick and Afflicted* (1989), pp. 19–20.

"God Provided a Helpmeet," from "I Stand All Amazed," in *As a Woman Thinketh* (Salt Lake City: Bookcraft, 1990), pp. 136–37.

"The Rocker," from *Bedtime Stories for Grownups* (Salt Lake City: Bookcraft, 1988), pp. 70–73.

"The Summers of My Life," from *The Seasoning* (Salt Lake City: Bookcraft, 1981), pp. 68–70.

"'I Loved Your Father,'" from *Mothering* (Salt Lake City: Bookcraft, 1993), pp. 42–43.

"Dirty Socks," from *Count Your Many Blessings* (Salt Lake City: Bookcraft, 1995), pp. 78–79.

Men and Women, Mothers and Fathers

"'I Am His Daughter,'" from the Seoul Area Conference, women's session.

"What Are You Going to Be?" from *Life—One to a Customer* (Salt Lake City: Bookcraft, 1981), pp. 115–17.

"A Girl's Best Friend," from *Mothering* (Salt Lake City: Bookcraft, 1993), p. 83.

"Reconciliation," from *Bedtime Stories for Grownups* (Salt Lake City: Bookcraft, 1988), pp. 3–5.

"Fathers and Sunshine," from *Sunshine* (Salt Lake City: Bookcraft, 1994), pp. 69–70.

"Fathers I Have Known," from *Sunshine* (Salt Lake City: Bookcraft, 1994), pp. 71–76.

"My Mother," from *Sunshine* (Salt Lake City: Bookcraft, 1994), pp. 7–9.

"A Thinking Woman," from "I Stand All Amazed," in *As a Woman Thinketh* (Salt Lake City: Bookcraft, 1990), p. 140.

"Father's Day," from *Life—One to a Customer* (Salt Lake City: Bookcraft, 1981), pp. 132–36.

"Mother: Look at You!" from *Mothering* (Salt Lake City: Bookcraft, 1993), pp. 1–4.

"'This Is How I'm Supposed to Be,'" *Ensign*, November 1979, pp. 106–7.

"Women As an Influence," from *Life—One to a Customer* (Salt Lake City: Bookcraft, 1981), pp. 20–23.

Do unto Others

"Allie and Tony," from *The Seasoning* (Salt Lake City: Bookcraft, 1981), pp. 28–31.

"The Magic of Cookie-Cutter Sandwiches," from *God*

Bless the Sick and Afflicted (Salt Lake City: Bookcraft, 1989), p. 40.

"My Neighbor! My Friend!" from *Sunshine for the Latter-day Saint Soul* (Salt Lake City: Bookcraft, 1998), pp. 33–34.

"The Kindness of Strangers," from *Sunshine* (Salt Lake City: Bookcraft, 1994), pp. 43–44.

"A Lot of Good People Out There," from *Life—One to a Customer* (Salt Lake City: Bookcraft, 1981), pp. 145–48.

"What Gift for You, My Friend?" from *Love You!* (Salt Lake City: Bookcraft, 1991), pp. 16–18.

"The Man from the Tavern," from *Count Your Many Blessings* (Salt Lake City: Bookcraft, 1995), pp. 116–17.

"God Bless the Sick and Afflicted," from *God Bless the Sick and Afflicted* (Salt Lake City: Bookcraft, 1989), pp. xi–xii.

"Helen Winget," from *God Bless the Sick and Afflicted* (Salt Lake City: Bookcraft, 1989), pp. 23–24.

"'I Needed to Do a Good Deed,'" from *God Bless the Sick and Afflicted* (Salt Lake City: Bookcraft, 1989), pp. 33–34.

"The Goodness of Man and of God," from *God Bless the*

Sick and Afflicted (Salt Lake City: Bookcraft, 1989), pp. 66–69.

"Winter Comes When the Heart Breaks," from *The Seasoning* (Salt Lake City: Bookcraft, 1981), pp. 3–10.

"A Christmas Eve Gift," from "Experiment on His Word," in Richard H. Cracroft and H. Wallace Goddard, *My Soul Delighteth in the Scriptures* (Salt Lake City: Bookcraft, 1999), pp. 129–30.

Love

"In Heaven with You," from *Love You!* (Salt Lake City: Bookcraft, 1991), pp. 8–9.

"At Baptism," from *Love You!* (Salt Lake City: Bookcraft, 1991), p. 102.

"Heaven's Fire," from *Love You!* (Salt Lake City: Bookcraft, 1991), pp. 39–40.

"Filled with Divine Love," from Elaine Cannon and Ed J. Pinegar, *Called to Serve Him* (Salt Lake City: Bookcraft, 1991), pp. 98–100.

"Walk in Love," from *Love You!* (Salt Lake City: Bookcraft, 1991), pp. 19–20.

"'She Needs You to Love Her,'" from *Merry, Merry Christmases* (Salt Lake City: Bookcraft, 1988), pp. 54–55.

"Love All People," from *Love You!* (Salt Lake City: Bookcraft, 1991), pp. 98–99.

"Honeycomb," from *Love You!* (Salt Lake City: Bookcraft, 1991), p. 124.

"Isn't Loving Wonderful?" from *Be a Bell Ringer* (Salt Lake City: Bookcraft, 1989), pp. 79–80.

"Peaceable Things," from *Love You!* (Salt Lake City: Bookcraft, 1991), pp. 142–43.

"Friends and Enemies," from *Love You!* (Salt Lake City: Bookcraft, 1991), pp. 130–33.

A Grateful Heart

"The Gift of Trouble," from *Life—One to a Customer* (Salt Lake City: Bookcraft, 1981), pp. 28–31.

"Forever Sunshine," from *Sunshine* (Salt Lake City: Bookcraft, 1994), pp. 123–24.

"A View from Above," from *Life—One to a Customer* (Salt Lake City: Bookcraft, 1981), pp. 24–27.

"'Thanks a Million!'" from *Life—One to a Customer* (Salt Lake City: Bookcraft, 1981), pp. 84–85.

"'Count Your Many Blessings,'" from *Count Your Many Blessings* (Salt Lake City: Bookcraft, 1995), pp. 155–56.

"'God Bless You,'" from *Merry, Merry Christmases* (Salt Lake City: Bookcraft, 1988), p. 31.

REFERENCES

"A Lesson in Gratitude," from *Mothering* (Salt Lake City: Bookcraft, 1993), pp. 23–24.

"Count Your Blessings and Abide," from *Adversity* (Salt Lake City: Bookcraft, 1987), p. 42.

"A Change in Attitude," from *Adversity* (Salt Lake City: Bookcraft, 1987), pp. 60–61.

"Name Them One by One," from *Sunshine* (Salt Lake City: Bookcraft, 1994), pp. 1–3.

In the Midst of Affliction

"Adversity Gives Us Experience," from *Adversity* (Salt Lake City: Bookcraft, 1987), pp. 39–41.

"'Make It a Good Day,'" from *Adversity* (Salt Lake City: Bookcraft, 1987), pp. 20–21.

"Finding Beauty amidst Trouble," from *God Bless the Sick and Afflicted* (Salt Lake City: Bookcraft, 1989), pp. 101–2.

"Adversity Proves Whom God Can Trust," from *Adversity* (Salt Lake City: Bookcraft, 1987), pp. 29–30.

"Returning Good for Evil," from *Count Your Many Blessings* (Salt Lake City: Bookcraft, 1995), pp. 94–96.

"The Great Ones Stretch above It," from *Adversity* (Salt Lake City: Bookcraft, 1987), p. 4.

REFERENCES

"For Our Eternal Good," from *Adversity* (Salt Lake City: Bookcraft, 1987), pp. 35–36.

"Come and Get It!" from *Adversity* (Salt Lake City: Bookcraft, 1987), pp. 111–13.

"Promises and Pink Carnations," from *God Bless the Sick and Afflicted* (Salt Lake City: Bookcraft, 1989), pp. 133–35.

"Hope Wipes Out Worry," from "Experiment on His Word," in Richard H. Cracroft and H. Wallace Goddard, *My Soul Delighteth in the Scriptures* (Salt Lake City: Bookcraft, 1999), pp. 132–34.

Through Humble Prayer

"Jesus Listening Can Hear," from *Sunshine* (Salt Lake City: Bookcraft, 1994), pp. 106–7.

"A Lesson in Faith," from *Count Your Many Blessings* (Salt Lake City: Bookcraft, 1995), pp. 100–2.

"'I Need Help,'" from *Count Your Many Blessings* (Salt Lake City: Bookcraft, 1995), pp. 103–4.

"The Pear Tree," from *Sunshine* (Salt Lake City: Bookcraft, 1994), pp. 101–2.

"Priesthood Blessings," from *Count Your Many Blessings* (Salt Lake City: Bookcraft, 1995), pp. 41–42.

"A Prayer for Our Home," from *Adversity* (Salt Lake City: Bookcraft, 1987), pp. 58–59.

"A Child's Prayer," from *Adversity* (Salt Lake City: Bookcraft, 1987), pp. 87–89.

"A Healing Blessing," from *God Bless the Sick and Afflicted* (Salt Lake City: Bookcraft, 1989), pp. 83–84.

"He Was Weeping," from *The Seasoning* (Salt Lake City: Bookcraft, 1981), pp. 56–57.

"Call upon the Elders," from *God Bless the Sick and Afflicted* (Salt Lake City: Bookcraft, 1989), pp. 84–86.

"Mark's Answer," from *God Bless the Sick and Afflicted* (Salt Lake City: Bookcraft, 1989), pp. 80–83.

"'I Want Each One to Pray,'" from "Experiment on His Word," in Richard H. Cracroft and H. Wallace Goddard, *My Soul Delighteth in the Scriptures* (Salt Lake City: Bookcraft, 1999), pp. 123–24.

Principles for Happy Days

"Those Who Sin Differently," from *Life—One to a Customer* (Salt Lake City: Bookcraft, 1981), pp. 6–8.

"On the Way to School," from *Bedtime Stories for Grownups* (Salt Lake City: Bookcraft, 1988), pp. 81–82.

"Knowledge Isn't Enough," from Elaine Cannon and Ed J. Pinegar, *Called to Serve Him* (Salt Lake City: Bookcraft, 1991), pp. 116–17.

"Self-Control," from *Life—One to a Customer* (Salt Lake
    City: Bookcraft, 1981), pp. 10–13.

"The Oleander," from *The Summer of My Content* (Salt
    Lake City: Deseret Book, 1976), pp. 7–8.

"When Blessings Turn into Burdens," from *Adversity* (Salt
    Lake City: Bookcraft, 1987), pp. 10–13.

"A Crushing Desire to Believe," from *God Bless the Sick
    and Afflicted* (Salt Lake City: Bookcraft, 1989), p. 58.

"A Near-Magic Survival System," from *God Bless the Sick
    and Afflicted* (Salt Lake City: Bookcraft, 1989), p. 138.

"Finding Value in a Torn and Tattered Book," from
    "Experiment on His Word," in Richard Cracroft and
    H. Wallace Goddard, *My Soul Delighteth in the
    Scriptures* (Salt Lake City: Bookcraft, 1999),
    pp. 125–27.

"Some Don'ts," from *God Bless the Sick and Afflicted* (Salt
    Lake City: Bookcraft, 1989), pp. 129–30.

A Choice Generation

"Celebrate Yourself," from *Not Just Ordinary Young Men
    and Young Women* (Salt Lake City: Bookcraft, 1991),
    pp. 25–30.

"You Are a Daughter of God," from *Be a Bell Ringer* (Salt
    Lake City: Bookcraft, 1989), pp. 27–30.

REFERENCES

"Youthful You," from *Heart to Heart* (Salt Lake City: Bookcraft, 1983), pp. 52–53.

"A Pearl of a Girl," from *Not Just Ordinary Young Men and Young Women* (Salt Lake City: Bookcraft, 1991), pp. 33–41.

"Someday," from *Heart to Heart* (Salt Lake City: Bookcraft, 1983), pp. 66–67.

"Satisfaction Guaranteed," from *Not Just Ordinary Young Men and Young Women* (Salt Lake City: Bookcraft, 1991), pp. 151–53.

"Choose to Stay Choice," from *Heart to Heart* (Salt Lake City: Bookcraft, 1983), pp. 78–79.

"A Tribute to Youth," from *Heart to Heart* (Salt Lake City: Bookcraft, 1983), p. 84.

"Give Me Five!" from *Heart to Heart* (Salt Lake City: Bookcraft, 1983), pp. 61–65.

"Talk It Over," from *Heart to Heart* (Salt Lake City: Bookcraft, 1983), pp. 90–91.

Angels and Miracles

"Angels and Peaceable Things," from *The Truth about Angels* (Salt Lake City: Bookcraft, 1996), pp. 1–4.

"'Almost!'" from *The Truth about Angels* (Salt Lake City: Bookcraft, 1996), pp. 10–11.

"An Angel Hovering over Us," previously unpublished.

REFERENCES

"To Be Known by God," from *The Truth about Angels* (Salt Lake City: Bookcraft, 1996), pp. 15–16.

"Heavenly Help," from *The Truth about Angels* (Salt Lake City: Bookcraft, 1996), pp. 17–19.

"Happy Birthday," from *The Truth about Angels* (Salt Lake City: Bookcraft, 1996), pp. 26–27.

"God Created Angels," from *The Truth about Angels* (Salt Lake City: Bookcraft, 1996), p. 43.

"A Command to Repent," from *The Truth about Angels* (Salt Lake City: Bookcraft, 1996), pp. 106–9.

INDEX

INDEX

channels of, 82–83

Peer pressure, responding to, 315–16

Pehrson, Mark and Diane, 338–40

Persecution, responding to, 212–15

Perspective: gaining a new perspective on your life, 179–83; ability of children to restore, 223–24

Peterson, H. Burke, 65

Prayer: importance of frequent prayer, 74–75; for the sick and afflicted, 117–19; asking to be directed to those in need, 119; listening for the still small voice, 123–24; in desperate circumstances, 124–27, 304–8; to help you accept God's will, 233–36; in times of adversity, 233–36; definition of, 234–35; in gratitude for priesthood blessings, 238–39; giving God the opportunity to help, 240–42; importance of faith, 242–46; as an admission of your need for God's help, 246; dedicating your home, 249–51; children's faith expressed in, 252–55; family, 258–59; humility in, 259; personal blessings of, 262; training children in, 266–68

Priesthood blessings: power of, 236–38, 260–62; in times of illness, 236–38, 255–57, 260–62, 291–92; gratitude for, 238–39; as an affirmation of God's interest in us, 246; for babies, 246–47; at confirmation, 247–48; when death is near, 248–49, 263–66; as a tool for learning, 255–57

Principles, correct, 290

Prodigal children: accepting the return of, 55–57; learning from the biblical parable, 57–59

Reconciliation: parents' role in, 55–57; as an expression of Christlike love, 57; prodigal son's father as the master of, 58–59

Rejection: being the last player chosen, 127–30; positive action vs. negative reaction, 131–32; suicide as a response to, 133–34

Richards, George F., 61

Richards, LeGrand, 62

Scripture study: power of, 36; in times of adversity, 225–29; as part of your "survival system," 289; family, 290–93

Self-control, 279–82

Seneca, 279

Service: to those who are grieving, 102–3; to those in trying circumstances, 104–5; to others when your own needs are great, 105–7, 139–42; from strangers, 105–7; to the defeated, 108–9; to the elderly, 109–10; to the sick and afflicted, 110–11, 112, 117–19, 120–21; to people with disabilities, 111–12; repaying, 112–13; from those we may be inclined to judge harshly, 116–17; as a way to unburden yourself, 121–23; in desperate circumstances, 124–27; as an expression of your love for Christ, 146, 147, 153–54; as part